Shifting the Spotlight in the Law of Rape

Shifting the Spotlight in the Law of Rape

The Responsibilities of Penetration

Jonathan Herring
Sorcha McCormack

ANTHEM PRESS

Anthem Press
An imprint of Wimbledon Publishing Company
www.anthempress.com

This edition first published in UK and USA 2026
by ANTHEM PRESS
75–76 Blackfriars Road, London SE1 8HA, UK
or PO Box 9779, London SW19 7ZG, UK
and
244 Madison Ave #116, New York, NY 10016, USA

British Library Cataloguing-in-Publication Data
A catalogue record for this book is available from the British Library.

Library of Congress Cataloging-in-Publication Data: 2025937200
A catalog record for this book has been requested.

ISBN-13: 978-1-83999-529-3 (Pbk)
ISBN-10: 1-83999-529-7 (Pbk)

This title is also available as an eBook.

To Bowie

CONTENTS

ACKNOWLEDGEMENTS

We are grateful to the team at Anthem Press, particularly Jebaslin Hephzibah, for their support and help during the writing of this book.

We have drawn on ideas from previous publications in developing this book (including, 'The Duties of Penetration and the Limits of Consent' [2024] *Criminal Law Review* 94; 'Is Affirmative Consent the Answer? Yes, Sort Of, Maybe' [2025] *Journal of Criminal Law*; 'Reforming Rape: From Consent to Responsibility' [2025] *Gender and Justice*. We are grateful to anonymous reviewers for their comments on those articles.

Jonathan is particularly grateful for the intellectual support and friendship of colleagues, especially Shazia Choudhry, Michelle Madden Dempsey, Rachel Taylor, Marthe Gouldsmit Samaritter, Imogen Goold and Heloise Robinson; with an extra special thanks to Hannah Bows, who introduced Sorcha and Jonathan. A special thank you to Sorcha, who is the perfect co-author. At home, Kirsten, Laurel, Jo and Darcy are loving and hilarious.

Sorcha is, as always, indebted to the incredible Beverly Clough for her continued encouragement, mentorship and boundless wisdom. On a personal level, I'm eternally grateful for my little girls, Croía and Bowie, who I hope to make proud in the work that I do. To my rock of a husband, Jonny, for always believing in me, and to my mother-in-law Julie, who, without her caring support during maternity leave, this would not have been possible. Finally, to Jonathan Herring, for his generosity, unreserved support and for making writing fun!

Chapter 1

INTRODUCTION

'I will be on the stand, I think I am on trial. I am on trial. They want me to stand up there and re-traumatise myself and speak about the most shaming and disgusting things. I am worried this is going to be the most traumatic, shaming, and humiliating thing in my life' (Rape Crisis 2024a, 1).

Rape Law is failing victims. Fewer and fewer are willing to report what they have gone through. Their experience of criminal trials is traumatic. While it is an exaggeration to say rape has been effectively decriminalised (Rape Crisis 2024), it's not much of an exaggeration (Equality Now 2017). Rape Law is in crisis.

According to the Office for National Statistics, there has been an increase in reported rape to the police. Where it is reported though only 2.6 per cent of cases result in prosecutions, with around two-thirds of those cases leading to a conviction. That suggests that between two and three out of every 1,000 rapes lead to a conviction. Even where there is a prosecution, as we shall see in Chapter 3, many rape trials appear to be more effective at re-traumatising victims than producing justice for them. In a damning indictment of the current legal response, a report by the Victim's Commissioner found that when survivors of sexual assault were asked if they thought victims could obtain justice by reporting to the police, just 5 per cent strongly agreed, and a further 9 per cent agreed (Molina and Poppleton, 2020, 4). It is hoped that recent improvements in police training around rape will improve the police response to rape.

There is a pandemic of rape. According to UN Women (2024), worldwide almost one in three women, around 736 million people 'have been subjected to physical and/or sexual intimate partner violence, non-partner sexual violence, or both at least once in their life (30 per cent of women aged 15 and older)'. The Crime Survey for England and Wales has estimated that in the year ending March 2022, 798,000 women experienced some form of sexual assault (ONS 2023). In July 2024, the National Policing statement claimed:

'Violence Against Women and Girls (VAWG) has reached epidemic levels in England and Wales, in terms of its scale, complexity and impact on victims. We have seen a 37% increase in recorded VAWG related crimes from 2018/19 to 2022/23'. Shockingly, in the year ending March 2024, the age group with the highest rate of reported rape was 14-year-old girls (Hymas 2024). A third of all reported rapes involved girls under the age of 18 (Hymas 2024).

To remedy the legal response to rape requires a broad range of interventions and changes. We need to challenge wider societal attitudes; online material; broader misogamy; education in schools; policing. The list goes on and on. In this book, we will focus on what role the legal definition of rape can play in improving things for victims. We fully accept that this alone will have only a limited impact. However, we think it is a key starting point. If we get the definition of rape correct, this will have a huge impact in terms of education, policing and wider societal attitudes.

The topic is controversial, and we have already entered the controversy by using the term 'victim'. There is controversy from two angles. First, many lawyers writing in this area use the term 'complainant' rather than 'victim'. This is preferred as it avoids any assumptions that the defendant is guilty and that a rape has taken place. The term 'complainant' acknowledges that someone has made a complaint without necessarily accepting that a rape has taken place. However, we use the term 'victim'. We note that in legal writing, the only offence in which the term 'complainant' (rather than 'victim') is used is rape. We do not talk of complainants of robbery, for example. The use of a special term in relation to rape seems to reflect a culture of disbelief and the myth that it is common for women to make up false allegations of rape. That is, in fact, untrue. There are no more false allegations of rape than any other offences (Scottish Government 2023). Further, it is not inappropriate to describe someone as a victim of rape, even if the defendant is not guilty of the crime (e.g. because they lack *mens rea* [the mental element of the crime]). The victim has been subjected to a non-consensual sexual act, something not captured by the label 'complainant'.

Second, among advocacy groups, the term 'survivor' rather than 'victim' is preferred. They argue that the term 'victim' connotes a passiveness: something has been done to them, reflecting a sense of weakness or powerlessness (Dunn 2005). Many can internalise the label 'victim', which can impact their ability to develop a new sense of self and overcome their trauma. Instead, 'survivor' is suggested to be empowering, redistributing the power from the perpetrator to them as people overcoming their abuse. Indeed, some research has shown that internalising the 'survivor' label has a more positive impact on mental well-being (Jagielski et al 2012). Further, the concept of 'victim' itself can be perceived narrowly and have heavy connotations with notions of the 'ideal' victim, where victims are expected to fit into a script or stereotype.

On this issue, we accept that language is a powerful tool; its impacts and meanings are also inherently subjective. We encourage victims of sexual violence to use the most appropriate terminology as they see fit (Larson 2018). In this book on the legal definition of rape, we use the term 'victim' as that fits with the legal terminology normally used when discussing criminal offences, while accepting in many other contexts 'survivor' might be more appropriate.

This book focuses on men's rape of women. Our focus is not to distract from the fact that males can be victims of sexual assault. Indeed in 2022, it was estimated that there were 75,000 male victims in England and Wales (ONS, 2023). However, there are often different factors at play in a male-male rape or female-male or female-female sexual assault. These deserve proper consideration in their own right and cannot be covered in a book of this size.

Chapter 2

PROBLEMS WITH THE LAW OF RAPE

The Current Definition of Rape

The Sexual Offences Act 2003 is now 22 years old and in desperate need of reform. The Act sets out the definition of rape in Section 1(1):

A person (A) commits an offence if –

(a) he intentionally penetrates the vagina, anus or mouth of another person (B) with his penis;
(b) B does not consent to the penetration; and
(c) A does not reasonably believe that B consents.

At the heart of this definition is that the prosecution must prove B (the victim) did not consent to the act. There is much that could be written about this definition of rape, including its focus on penile penetrations and its gendered nature. In this book, our focus is on the place of consent in the offence.[1]

The Confusing Law on Consent

Consent is defined in Section 74 in this way:

[...] a person consents if he agrees by choice, and has the freedom and capacity to make that choice.

The difficulty with this definition is that without more being said, it begs as many questions as it answers. How much pressure must be experienced before a person is not 'free'? What level of understanding is required if a person is to have capacity? If someone is intoxicated, does this mean they lack the ability to make a choice? How must the 'agreement' be expressed? As the statute gives little answer to these questions, much can be made of the fact the

---

1 We will not, therefore, in this book discuss whether there should be a distinction between a penile sexual penetration and a penetration with something else.

concept of consent is unclear, and therefore the jury cannot be sure beyond reasonable doubt that the victim did not consent.

While the legislation includes rebuttable and conclusive presumptions around the existence of consent in Sections 75 and 76, these seem to have done little to improve clarity, indeed they have added to the confusion. We take one example. Under Section 75, the jury should be instructed that if it is proved that 'any person had administered to or caused to be taken by the complainant, without the complainant's consent, a substance which, having regard to when it was administered or taken, was capable of causing or enabling the complainant to be stupefied or overpowered at the time of the relevant act' and that the defendant knew this, then the jury should conclude that the victim did not consent to the act, unless the defendant adduces 'sufficient evidence […] to raise an issue as to whether [the victim] consented'. Where such evidence is introduced, the presumption is rebutted and the jury should return to the question of whether the victim consented, beyond reasonable doubt, considering all the evidence available. If you are not familiar with the provision, you would have needed to have read this paragraph several times to understand it and that is with our best attempt to present it as clearly as possible. These presumptions are hard enough to explain to a group of law students, let alone a jury.

Not only is the law hard to explain, the message it sends is confusing. This is particularly apparent with the use of rebuttable presumptions. Through a guise of clarification and protection, Section 75 sets out the circumstances in which it is presumed that an individual is not consenting, unless additional evidence can be adduced to demonstrate otherwise. The circumstances covered by Section 75 include where a victim:

a)   is subject to or fears immediate violence against themselves;
b)   is subject to or fears immediate violence against another person;
c)   unlawfully detained and the defendant was not;
d)   was asleep or unconscious;
e)   was physically disabled and could not communicate consent; and
f)   was involuntarily intoxicated (as above mentioned).

The difficulty with these rebuttable presumptions is that they appear to send mixed messages. In these circumstances, there may be not be consent, but there may be (if evidence is introduced there was). However, with many of these circumstances, the message should be much clearer. If the victim was asleep or cannot communicate consent,[2] these are not cases where the law

---

2 Those with a mental disability or 'disorder' are placed within Section 30 and offered further additional protections.

should indicate there is arguably no consent, there should be a clear message of no consent. Particularly striking is a case where the defendant is aware that the victim has been given a stupefying substance (such as alcohol or Rohypnol) without her consent (cases of so-called spiking; Stephenson et al (2023)). In such a case, we cannot imagine a scenario where a defendant should be able to claim that the victim consented. More fundamentally the law fails to provide clear guidance to the public. The message should be clear: if you know your would-be partner has had her drink spiked or is otherwise involuntarily intoxicated you should not have sex with her. Instead, the law can be read as indicating that if there is any kind of consent the victim did consent, then the defendant can proceed without fear of a criminal conviction. This is because a rape will only be found to occur where it is beyond reasonable doubt that the victim was not consenting. That we think is a dangerous and undesirable message to send. It is particularly problematic as victims of spiking are often unable to remember the events and so dispute what D claims to have happened (Stephenson et al 2024).

Three Particular Problems with Consent

In this section, we highlight three particular problems with the law on consent in rape. Plenty more could be provided, but the focus of this book is on making the case for a new law, rather than picking out the problems with the current formulation.

First, our major concern is that when a jury decides whether there is consent, they are often influenced by stereotypes and myths. We will be looking at these later in Chapter 3, but they focus on issues such as the clothes the victim was wearing, the response of the victim to the incident and their previous sexual history. While it might be thought unlikely that a jury member would fall for the crude line that 'the victim must have consented to sex because she was wearing a short skirt', it should be recalled that the jury need to be persuaded that 'beyond reasonable doubt' there was no consent. A skilled barrister can use these myths to introduce at least a doubt in a jury's mind. They do not need the jury to adopt the myth hook line and sinker. The failure to provide detailed guidance on what counts as consent means these myths are given scope to be misused by a defence barrister.

Second, whether due to rape myths, or other reasons, there are shocking examples of where juries appear to have found there was consent, despite that being unlikely. Indeed, the requirement that the lack of consent be proved beyond reasonable doubt means in effect the sexual availability of women is presumed. In the absence of violence, juries seem to struggle to find it proved that there was no consent. In *R v. Gardner* (2005), a girl aged 14 was found to have consented to a digital penetration by a 19-year-old man. At the time of the penetration, she had drunk a considerable amount of alcohol and was being sick into a toilet. The appellant came into the bathroom while she was being sick, pulled down her trousers and digitally penetrated her. As she was under the age of consent, the defendant was still convicted of an offence, but was sentenced on the basis that the victim had in fact consented. It was accepted that she was 'taken advantage of', but the lack of consent had not been proved. But the finding of consent is absurd. This is one of a long line of cases where courts have been willing to accept that intoxicated victims have consented in circumstances where it is unlikely to have been given (Finch and Munro 2005; Clough 2019). The particular difficulty is that where the victim cannot remember the incident (which is very likely in a case of a high degree of intoxication), this is taken to mean it cannot be shown she did not consent (*R v. Dougal* 2005). The difficulty with these cases is the fact the burden is seen as lying on the victim to prove the absence of consent. Proving the absence beyond reasonable doubt of something is obviously a very difficult task.

Another striking example of this are rough sex cases, where the defendant has killed the victim and successfully claims that this was 'rough sex' gone wrong. As Bows and Herring (2022) have illustrated, many of these have involved horrific violence and yet courts have accepted there was consent. Of course, in such cases, the victim is not able to give evidence to dispute the defendant's story. Nevertheless, the willingness to accept that this was consensual violence is extraordinary. If even in such blatant cases, juries and courts cannot see the lack of consent; there is something seriously wrong with the use of consent in sexual offences (Herring 2022).

Our third point is that the law fails to take victim's sexual autonomy seriously. In *R v. Lawrance* (2020), the defendant lied to the victim and told her he was infertile as he had had a vasectomy and she fell pregnant. The court overturned the conviction on appeal finding that her consent was still valid despite the intentional deception. We explore the issues raised by this case further in Chapter 5, Section 'Consent and Mistake', but it is striking that even though the victim's consent was not full, nor informed, and she was absolutely misled, it was not shown to indicate a lack of consent. The issue of her partner's potency was crucial to her consent, but the court determined it was not sufficiently serious to negate consent. It may well be that an excessive focus on the existence of consent, in its most basic terms, has led to this conclusion. In particular, this case highlights how the focus of the law can too often be on whether a 'yes' was given by the victim, rather than looking at the circumstances within which the 'yes' was given, and whether it represented a genuine attempt by the defendant to determine whether the victim consented. Or even an attempt to ascertain what it was the victim was saying 'yes' to.

A further example of this point is *R (on the application of Monica) v. DPP* (2018), the defendant was an undercover police officer who had infiltrated an environmental activist group and withheld his true identity. The victim claimed she would not have consented had she known the officer's true identity, but the court found that his deception did not undermine the consent she had given. Again, we would disagree with this decision, indeed the issues with this decision become even more apparent when we consider what the defendant knew. With a focus on the defendant, we might question his awareness and note that the deception was intentionally used to obtain consent, with blatant disregard for the victim's autonomy.

The problems with the current definition of rape become all the more apparent when we explore the experience of victims in rape trials. We turn to this in the next chapter.

Chapter 3

PROBLEMS WITH RAPE TRIALS

Few lawyers are happy with the way rape trials work. They are, as they usually are in criminal cases, adversarial. The lawyer for the prosecution tries to pin blame on the defendant and the lawyer for the defence trying to persuade the jury that the victim has lied or misremembered. The defence lawyer's task is to do their very best to introduce doubt about the victim's version of events, because if the jury are not sure beyond reasonable doubt about the defendant's guilt they must acquit. It is not surprising that victims who have been subjected to cross-examination describe it as 'judicial rape' (Lees 2002, 36) and 'rape of the second kind' (Matoesian 1995, 676). Having suffered the indignity of a rape, it is now claimed by a person in an official setting that in fact they wanted the intercourse to occur or they have misremembered what has happened. This, in other contexts, would be regarded as gaslighting (Sweet 2019).

Difficulties for Victims Pre-Trial

The challenges faced by victims of rape begin long before the trial. As we noted in Chapter 1, very few cases of alleged rape reach trial, with many victims deciding not to report the offence or not to continue supporting the prosecution. There are many reasons for this. Some reflect the impact of rape myths on the victim themselves, others reflect the attitudes of investigators and prosecutors. The first stage may see victims blaming themselves, questioning their own actions, what they did or didn't do to avoid the assault and potentially trivialising or disregarding their own experience. Later, if a victim accepts they were assaulted, they may fear they will be judged, preventing them from reporting or confiding in another person. If victims do report their assault to the police, they may then be met by suspicion from investigators, critically analysing their behaviour, clothing and scrutinising whether their response was *rational*. If their case happens to be one of the few that does go to Court, victims may be subject to further scrutiny where barristers, judges and jurors may rely on preconceived ideas of what rape is and how a *normal* person might respond. We therefore can conclude that myths and adverse attitudes have the potential to substantially and adversely impact a victim at every stage, therefore significantly contributing to the justice gap.

A particular problem at the moment is the huge backlog in rape cases. The average rape trial takes over two years to reach court (Rape Crisis 2024). Between 2019 and the end of 2023, there was a 346 per cent increase in the number of rape trials in the crown court backlog. The Chief Inspector of the CPS suggests that the number, currently at over 70,000, will soon reach 100,000 (Helm 2025). The government's plans to fast-track rape cases to deal with the backlog have proved challenging to implement (Helm 2025). The impact of these delays on victims is serious. Mary Glidon MP (2024) put it well in a recent debate in parliament:

> These are women and girls who are sitting at the feet of trauma. Survivors face the enormous challenge of having to relive their experiences in court, and each day until then. The lengthy delays, which can be anywhere from two to five years, draw out this experience. I fear that more and more women and girls are losing faith in our criminal justice system—a system that is supposed to protect them.

These delays seriously exacerbate the trauma for the victim and make it even easier for the cross-examination to suggest that, after all the time that has passed, the victim will not fully remember what happened. They also must cause many victims to decide they no longer want to continue assisting the prosecution.

The investigation and trial process itself is burdensome and often traumatising for the victim. A recent report, *Suffering for Justice*, exposed the extent of the problems experienced by victims of sexual violence (Victim Support 2024). The research was based on 12 semi-structured interviews of victim-survivors' experiences of the trial process after a defendant had been charged. It highlighted the severe and last-minute delays, unwanted and traumatising encounters with the defendant, problems accessing special measures and poor communication with victim-survivors. All of these had a significant impact on their mental well-being. The report also highlighted a 'post code lottery' where victim-survivors' access to special measures and support available varied tremendously between different parts of the country. The positive impact of the constant and consistent support from sexual violence support advisers was highly valued by all participants. It seems overall, from the report, that victim-survivors appear to feel lost in the criminal justice system. The communication is scant, incomplete and often delayed, with little to no explanations regarding sentencing. The report makes five key demands for change, and these include:

1) Listening to the needs of victim-survivors and to consistently deliver on their existing obligations and guidance, particularly within the Victims' Code.
2) Urgent action is required to minimise delays and adjournments and ensure timely communication of any adjournments.
3) Demanding that the CPS review the use and abuse of rape myths and sexual history evidence.
4) The role of Independent Sexual Violence Advisers (ISVAs) should be recognised in guidance and enabled in practice at each stage of the criminal justice process.

Protections for Victims at Trial

Fear about the experience of trial can lead victims to decide to withdraw from the prosecution. In response, Sections 23–30 of the Youth Justice and Criminal Evidence Act 1999 contain special measures to protect vulnerable victims giving testimony. These include giving evidence via video link, using pre-recorded interviews and screening the witness box to prevent the witness from seeing the accused. Although such measures offer the prospect of some-what mitigating the negative impact of the trial process, *Suffering for Justice* found that many victims are made to feel as though they should not access these provisions, as the jury would look unfavourably on them for doing so (Victim Support 2024). Likewise, some victims found that their requests were denied due to the lack of technology. In one case, someone was told they couldn't be screened because the screen was being used in another courtroom.

It would therefore appear that whilst in law, there are some measures in place to offer vulnerable victims additional protections, in practice these are not fulfilled. Likewise, despite victims identifying the presence of Independent Sexual Violence Advisors or ISVA's as crucial for their well-being, it was noted that their presence was also dissuaded by barristers: 'The barristers will say, "We don't feel it looks good to the jury if you've got an ISVA in there with you"'.

Cross-Examination

Another key theme that appeared in most interviews with victim-survivors was the use of inappropriate lines of questioning and reliance on stereotypical myths to undermine their credibility:

> She [defence barrister] was implying a lot of the time that I had made it
> up [...] and she asked me what I was wearing and that really didn't sit
> right with me because I don't think it's about that at all. At my interview
> [with the police], I was asked what I was wearing [...] So I feel like, the
> way that she [defence barrister] made it out like I was doing something
> to provoke him [...] Some of the questions were a bit far. She was almost
> victim-blaming, in a way, which made me look really angry.

> 'I was sat in the Section 28 room and, pretty much, for about two hours
> just the prosecutor I think, the defendant's one, just said, 'This is what
> happened, you're lying aren't you?' Everything that he said was about
> how I lied about it [...] It was just really, really, hard to hear someone
> say all that when it's not true. It kind of felt like I was the one on trial,
> to be honest.'

In a case where it is often 'he said v she said', the character of the victim often
becomes key to the jury deliberation. To win a case, a defence barrister simply has to persuade the jury that there is a reasonable doubt over the victim's
testimony. It is not surprising, therefore, that victims often feel that they are
under the spotlight in a rape trial, and many of the questions centre on the
blameworthiness or truthfulness of the victim (Gathings and Parrotta 2013;
McGlynn 2018; Ellison and Munro 2009). The Report's analysis showed that
at least one question based on myths or stereotypes was asked in 73 per cent
of the cases, including:

> 27% of victim-survivors were asked about what they did to prevent the
> offence; one-third were asked what they did to stop the offence while it
> was happening; one-third were asked if pursuing justice was a way of
> seeking revenge; and one-third were asked if they were under the influ-
> ence of alcohol or another substance.

Other victim-survivors were asked about their medication and mental health.
Any perceived flaw in the evidence or character of the victim is picked on and
exaggerated during the cross-examination.

Rape myths and stereotypical assumptions come in all shapes and sizes.
Some of the most prominent misconceptions include false allegations, 'asking
for it' through clothing, behaviour or intoxication, and 'real' rape myths that
deny acquaintance rapes and assume a woman would physically resist an
assault (Law Commission 2023). Even before a case gets to trial, these rape
myths can have a significant impact on how police respond to complaints. A
recent study by Sinclair (2022) showed a 'culture of scepticism' amongst police
officers. They appeared to prioritise cases which they deemed most likely to

secure a conviction, endorsing myths that a jury might be persuaded by in their decision-making.

While it might be too cynical to suggest that a victim will be portrayed as consenting unless she ensures she is dressed in a highly conservative way; never smiles or jokes; avoids drinking any alcohol; and never socialises, there is certainly much truth in the claim that a rape conviction is more likely where the victim is seen as a 'good victim'. As Mary Morgan (2024, 1) puts it:

> In allegations of sexual assault, there exists an 'ideal victim.' A good girl. Someone pure. The embodiment of virtuous. The personification of innocence [...] The ideal victim is a culmination of myths and false representations. It destroys the legitimacy of very real rape allegations and of survivors. It exonerates perpetrators. It blames and shames victims. It can singlehandedly prevent justice. And it is deployed constantly. Every victim who steps forward is examined with the lens of whether she is ideal.

In a major study by the Crown Prosecution Service on public understandings of rape concluded:

> The research showed that, overall, the public's accurate understanding of rape is outweighed by false beliefs, misunderstanding, lack of knowledge, and underlying stereotypes

They highlighted as particularly prevalent the belief that women often make up rape allegations and that rape was normally perpetrated by a stranger. Generally, over half those questioned either agreed with rape misconceptions or were unsure. Surprisingly, belief in the misconceptions were particularly prevalent among those 18–24. The Report went on to state:

> Overall, clear themes emerged showing that the public continue to hold narratives around stranger rape as the primary model for rape, beliefs about what 'real rape' looks like, how victims should behave, and a tendency to want to either exonerate the accused, find reasons for their actions, or set them apart from 'ordinary' men. And many of the assumptions and misconceptions have moved into the digital age, for example surrounding the behaviour of victims on-line.

Past Sexual History of the Victim

One issue which is particularly prominent is the sexual history of the victim. The implication that is commonly used is that because she agreed to sex on previous occasions, she may have consented to the sex subject to the charge (Connaghan and Russell, 2023). Perhaps surprisingly studies looking at public attitudes and mock juries suggest that such an argument is successful, at least in raising a doubt about the victim's testimony (Ellison and Munro 2009). Despite statutory attempts to limit the use of the evidence, it is still commonly presented. Sections 41–43 of the Youth Justice and Criminal Evidence Act 1999 were introduced following sustained criticism of the approach to sexual history evidence in sexual offence cases. Section 41(1) provides that, except with leave of the court, no evidence may be adduced at trial, and no question may be asked in cross-examination, by or on behalf of the defendant about any 'sexual behaviour' of the complainant. Gateways or exceptions, as detailed in Section 41(2) of the Youth Justice and Criminal Evidence Act 1999, need to be met in order to introduce the sexual history of the victim as evidence. In addition, the court must be satisfied that there is a risk the conviction would be unsafe if the evidence was not admitted. The exceptions are broad, vague and open to interpretation, often with the defendant's right to a fair trial as the underpinning logic for its admission. The wide and excessive use of sexual history evidence is currently being reviewed by the Law Commission (2023). The use of sexual history evidence has been abused for too long, and it is completely damaging and distracting to the case at hand.

As McGlynn (2018, 222) points out, in the context of sexual offences cases, the victim's sexual history 'contributes to shifting the focus of the trial from the defendant's actions to those of the complainant, thereby also shifting legal and moral blame and responsibility from the defendant to the complainant'. We advocate against the use of sexual history evidence in almost all circumstances. As it is in very rare circumstances, it could possibly bare relevance on the defendant's awareness of consent to the sexual activity in question. Consent to sex is consent to a particular act at a particular time with a particular person under particular circumstances with all relevant information communicated between the parties. A defendant should not be allowed to suggest that the fact the victim had previously agreed to sex (whether with the defendant or another person) gave him reasonable grounds to believe she was consenting to sex with him. The law should not be complicit in reinforcing these myths, and instead should require defendants to ensure rich consent is active and ongoing for the entire encounter.

A study undertaken by Temkin et al. (2018) revealed that the use of myths by defence barristers is still 'well-entrenched'. Tactics include highlighting to juries delays in the report of the assault; internet usage by the victim; her behaviour during the rape; and 'inconsistencies' in her evidence

(Law Commission 2023; Helm 2023). The experience of many survivors was captured by this comment:

> I was terrified upset and was asked inappropriate questions by the defence to things that I did not believe happened it was manipulated and crude and I felt attacked again. (Molina and Poppleton 2020, 46)

These efforts attempt to undermine victims' credibility and in essence, over-simplify how individuals might respond to an assault. By focusing on rational reactions and consistent approaches that in fact ignore the nuanced and situational variables of a sexual assault, victims' responses are undermined. As Smith and Skinner (2017, 458) state, myths are used as a form of 'rational ideal'.

The use of past sexual history is just one tactic used by defence barristers. Another is to focus on the intoxication of the victim.

Victims and Intoxication

Studies have shown the effect alcohol can have on the outcome of a case. It seems from research that women who are drunk at the time of the assault are held more responsible and blameworthy (Sims et al 2007). If a woman cannot control her actions, she tends to be viewed in a derogatory way (Richardson and Campbell 1982). Her character is viewed less favourably, she is less credible (Schuller and Stewart 2000) and she appears to be assigned more responsibility for her behaviour (Ellisson and Munro 2009, 2010).

Rape myths appear particularly impactful in cases where the victim was intoxicated at the time of the offence. It seems that those who apparently *chose* to become incapacitated at the time of the offence are deemed to have contributed to their exploitation (Finch and Munro 2005). Equally, many public campaigns 'to protect' women appear to have a similar message underpinned by autonomy and responsibilisation. Campaigns encourage women to avoid harm by avoiding so-called risky situations and to take responsibility for themselves. For example, Munro (2017) references several different campaigns that highlight this responsibilisation. In particular, Sussex Police's poster campaign questioned 'which one of your friends is most vulnerable'? Followed by the answer, 'the one you leave behind'; the use of 'vulnerable' here is applied 'simply by consequence of their being female and out in public'. (Munro 2017). In 2018, Devon and Cornwall police launched a #spike aware campaign, introducing drink spiking kits into bars and night clubs. Although a positive step to help identify the symptoms of drink spiking, the posters associated with the campaign have clear connotations of responsibilisation. For example, one such poster states '[d]rink spiking can lead to drowsiness, confusion and vulnerability – don't be a victim!' (Devon and Cornwall Police 2018). Similarly, in 2012, West Mercia police launched a poster campaign, communicating that intoxication makes young women vulnerable to rape, and also that the victim's contributory responsibility in getting drunk before any sexual attack should occasion retrospective regret (Munro 2008, 426).[1] Meanwhile, this instilled fear of women's perpetual risk of sexual assault ensures a vulnerable condition that must be managed diligently – by not drinking and limiting social activities – if she is to avoid condemnation for a contributory role in her victimisation (Munro 2018, 430). The reiteration of the need to stay safe keeps women in a 'constant state of fear' (Brownmiller 1975, 15) and has been argued as a 'weapon men use to perpetuate their dominance of women' (Frey and Douglas 1992). Hence, any sign of 'independence by women is often interpreted as asking to be raped' (Frey and Douglas 1992, 246); similarly, it is often endorsed that if a 'man wanted her she must have wanted him' (MacKinnon 1989, 330). Similar messages have been shared in Canada. For example, a police force released a statement encouraging women to 'avoid dressing like sluts in order not to be victimised'. (Savauger et al 2013, 631) Munro (2017, 426) rightly contends, such campaigns and beliefs are based on gender stereotypes of women as sexual gatekeepers and men as sexual predators with the responsibility of avoiding sexual assault 'borne heavily by the woman'.

Differentiation in Treatment

The final point we wish to emphasise in this chapter is the inequality in the treatment of the defendant and victim here. Any perceived flaw in the victim's character; any misremembered fact, any departure from the 'ideal' victim can be enough to demonstrate that there is doubt whether the defendant is guilty. This is particularly apparent in relation to intoxication. The drunkenness of the defendant is, if anything, seen as evidence in his favour; misunderstandings of the defendant are presented as reasonable mistakes in the heat of the moment; and past criminal behaviour is rarely admissible (Craig 2018). It appears that some people blame a man less if he is intoxicated at the time of the assault. His behaviour is usually forgiven due to his 'unintentional behaviour'; he is so intoxicated that he is unable to control his actions (Pollard 1992). It seems that no matter whether a man is drunk (too intoxicated to be blameworthy) or tipsy (blame the woman for being seductive) or sober

---

1 West Mercia Police later apologised: BBC (2012).

(more credible), there is always some excuse available from society to accept his behaviour (Ellison and Munro 2013). It therefore appears there is a general reluctance to label intoxicated non-consensual cases as rape. This attitude creates a 'double standard', whereby 'women are blamed more for a sexual assault offence when they have consumed alcohol [...] and the defendants are viewed less likely to have perpetrated the crime' (Gunby et al 2012).

Chapter 4

RETHINKING THE ETHICAL AND LEGAL FRAMEWORK AROUND RAPE

Sexual Penetration as a Prima Facie Wrong

A foundational claim for this book is this: when a man sexually penetrates a woman, he commits a prima facie legal wrong. That sounds a very surprising claim to many. We will justify it below, but before doing that it is worth clarifying two points about what we are saying. The first is that our claim is that a penile penetration is a *prima facie* wrong.[1] That means it is a wrong that calls for a justification. Where there is a justification, the act may be *all things considered* permissible, even good and excellent. Where there is no adequate justification, the act will be all things considered wrong. Explaining this with an example elsewhere may help. If Alfred were to push Barbara over, that would be prima facie wrong. Alfred could be appropriately called to account and explain why he acted as he did. Alfred may have a good explanation: 'Barbara was about to be hit by a car and I was saving her from an accident'. In that case, we may conclude that 'all things considered' his act was justified. Indeed, we might well say positively good. On the other hand, Alfred may not have a good explanation: 'I enjoy pushing people over and that is why I did it'. That would not be a good justification, and so 'all things considered' that would be a wrong. Similarly, if Alfred had no explanation for what he did ('I don't know why I did that'), the conclusion would be that all things considered he had committed a wrong.

Second, we repeat a point made in the Introduction. While we are discussing here a man sexually penetrating a woman, many of the same arguments could arise with a man sexually penetrating another man or a whole range of different sexual acts between different genders. There is no space to go through all these alternatives, and so we focus on a man sexually penetrating

---

1 Some writers use the term 'pro tanto' incorrectly.

a woman; however, it should be relatively straightforward to see how the argument can be used in other contexts.

So why do we say that a sexual penetration is a prima facie wrong? To answer this, it is worth thinking a bit more about how we might classify a prima facie wrong. It is an act that calls for a justification. In other words, it is something that is a wrong to another, for which a justification is required. So, whistling in the street is not a prima facie wrong. No explanation is required. Another way of thinking about this is to consider whether it is the kind of act for which it would be appropriate to ask for consent. We would not expect the person whistling in the street to check that those around them consent. We do, however, expect doctors and others to ask for consent before touching someone. That already provides one strong argument for why a sexual penetration is a prima facie wrong. It is something for which consent is required if it is to be justified.

With those points in mind, we can turn to establishing the claim that a sexual penetration is a prima facie wrong. The argument was first put forward by Michelle Madden Dempsey and Jonathan Herring. They claimed:

> When a man penetrates a woman's anus or vagina, he commits a prima facie moral wrong. Sexual penetration requires a justification, and in the absence of a justification, it will be wrong all things considered. (Madden Dempsey and Herring 2007, 467)

A detailed justification for that claim can be found in the original article, but the claim was based on the identification of three wrongs. The first two of which are nearly always present in male-on-female penetration, and the last one of which always is. Those three wrongs are as follows.

First, a sexual penetration involves the use of force against a body.[2] This is precisely the kind of act for which consent is typically expected. Jesse Wall (2015) writes that 'penetration of the vagina or anus, forceful or otherwise, is the use and control by the other, rather than the use and control by the self and hence a prima facie wrong'. A person who uses force against another and can offer no justification would be seen as acting wrongly.

The second wrong is that there are non-trivial risks of harm that are very often associated with penetrative sex (e.g., sexually transmitted diseases,

---

2 It is possible to imagine a case of male-on-female penetration where there is no force, for example, where the woman, rather than the man, does all the movement. In such a case, this basis for the wrong does not exist.

unwanted pregnancy; abrasions and bruising; and particularly the risk of psychological harm).[3] To expose another to such risks requires a good reason.

The third wrong is the negative social meaning that male penetration of a woman communicates in our society.[4] The message conveyed is 'the devaluation of women qua women and a disrespecting of women's humanity' (Madden Dempsey and Herring (2007, 486)), with which heterosexual sexual penetration is unfortunately always associated in a society marked by rape culture and sexism. As Madden Dempsey and Herring (2007, 486-7) put it:

> any credible interpretation of the practices of language regarding, and depictions of sexual penetration in our culture betray a social meaning of sexual penetration which devalues women *qua* women and disrespects women's humanity to an extent which renders such conduct prima facie wrong.

Sexual penetrations in themselves are using another person as a 'sexual object', and justification is required to ensure that that meaning or message is not conveyed (Morgan 2021, 527).

To these arguments, we would add two more.

The first is that, as argued above, the fact that we require consent for an act to be ethically justifiable is an automatic indicator that an act is a prima facie wrong which requires justification. Sexual penetrations are a paradigm example of an act for which consent is required. Consent does not need to be sought for acts which are not prima facie wrongful. Consent is required for acts which, lacking consent, or some other justification, are wrong. If there is nothing wrong with the act, no explanation is required of it. As Terrance McConnell (2019) argues that where consent has force, it 'gives a second person permission to do what would otherwise be wrong'. This is how consent operates in criminal law. The fact that consent is required in law is an indicator that legally the act is wrong. Consent releases D from a legal duty not to perform an act (Dougherty 2021a). The law quite properly rules that we should not use force on others' bodies; that is a legal duty which can be waived by consent.

The second is that it is commonly claimed that it is a sexual penetration without consent which is a prima facie wrong, not the sexual penetration

---

3 Again there may, occasionally, be cases where all these risks could be mitigated to such an extent that they do not apply, although that will be very rare.

4 Here there may be a difference if the sexes are different. We very much doubt that generally a woman sexually penetrating another woman conveys the negative social message discussed.

itself. While we agree that a sexual penetration without consent is a prima facie wrong, it should be noted that the 'without consent' is the absence of something. If one agrees that a sexual penetration without consent is a prima facie wrong, it seems odd to deny that the sexual penetration itself is not a prima facie wrong. Why should the lack of something (consent) be sufficient to change the moral character of the behaviour from morally unproblematic to being a prima facie wrong?

Kate Greasley (2021) has written powerfully against the claim that a sexual penetration is a prima facie wrong. At the core of her claim is that a prima facie wrongful act is one that should be regretted even if it is justified. The surgeon who has cut a patient open to remove a tumour has committed a prima facie wrong which has been justified. However, a justified wrong is one that should be avoided if at all possible. The surgeon has a duty to only perform such an operation if it is the only way to remove the tumour, and there should be a 'lingering regret' that there was not a less invasive way of removing the tumour. These are two core features of a justified wrong. We agree. Greasley argues that as these do not apply to sexual penetration, it would be incorrect to say that a sexual penetration is a prima facie wrong. While we agree with Greasley that it would be misguided to say sexual penetration must be avoided if there is a less wrongful way of achieving the good of penetration, with the result that 'people should strive toward celibacy, the way that many people strive to cut their carbon emissions or reduce their meat consumption'. Further, we agree that in the case of consensual sex, there should not be a lingering regret in connection with the act. However, neither concession requires us to conclude that a sexual penetration is not a prima facie wrong.

We say that for two reasons. First, what should be avoided in the case of a prima facie wrong are the aspects of the act that are wrongful. We do think that it is appropriate to say that the wrongful aspects identified above: the risks associated with sexual penetration and the negative social meaning should be avoided. The justification provided by consent is a way to avoid many of these. So, it is not sexual penetration per se that is to be avoided, but the wrongs associated with the act per se that are. Even with a justified consensual justified sex, we have reason to regret those matters which generate the prima facie wrongfulness, such as the negative social meaning. We long for a day when a sexual penetration will not inevitably be linked to being a tool of abuse, but can just be associated with loving acts.

Second, we suggest that there is an important distinction between the ways a justification can operate. Sometimes the justification puts up an alternate good which outweighs the harm caused. This is the case in surgery where the harm of the operation is outweighed by the good of its outcome. In such a case, we might regret that there was not a less wrongful way of achieving that good. However, in the case of justified sexual penetration, it is not that there is a good which outweighs the harm of penetration. Rather, the consent removes an important part of wrongfulness. A justified sexual penetration is not using another's body. There is then nothing in the justified penetration itself which should be regretted (Healey 2019). On this view (what Greasley (2021) calls 'the transformative effect of consent'), there is nothing to be regretted in justified sex because the wrongfulness has been removed. But Greasley responds with a powerful riposte:

> if the general reason against sexual penetration is completely extinguished in conditions of consent, then the obvious reply is that this general reason simply will not apply in the first place to consensual sex.

This means, she claims, that not all sexual penetrations require a justification, only those that are non-consensual.

We have two responses to Greasley's argument. The first is that we reject the claim that consent completely distinguishes all the arguments against a sexual penetration. Greasley's response only works for those whose sole argument for a sexual penetration relies on the use of the body. Indeed, as Quill R. Kukla (2018, 72) points out, consent 'is never going to be sufficient to make sex go well – we can consent to all sorts of lousy sex, including demeaning, boring, alienated, and unpleasantly painful or otherwise harmful sex'. Rather, as Madden Dempsey (2013) explains:

> If Amy has a reason not to punch Ben because doing so will cause Ben pain, Ben's consent provides Amy with a permission to exclude pain-based reasons from the reasons that bear on the moral quality of her action. It might still be unjustifiable for Amy to punch Ben, but if she takes up the exclusionary permission stemming from Ben's consent, then the pain-based reasons are excluded from her rational horizons.
>
> Ben's consent is no reason for Amy to punch Ben, but it can contribute to making Amy's punching Ben justifiable.

What is, therefore, still to be regretted in a case of justified penetration is the negative social meaning that the act attracts.

The second point is that there is a major difference between an act which is in no sense harmful to another (such as the whistling example above) and acts which are harmful to another, but for which they have consented (such as an ear piercing). In lumping together 'consensual sex' and 'whistling' as acts which are morally in the same camp, this distinction is lost. We return to the point above that a sexual penetration requires consent, specifically because of the harms attached to it. While, therefore, part of the usefulness of the prima facie wrong category is to indicate when there should be lingering regret, a more important aspect is in indicating to people what actions require consent. So, when Greasley states that 'consensual penetrative sex is conduct which [...] does not stand in need of justification', we disagree. Stating that penetrative consent requires justification sends the core message that it needs consent to be justified. Consensual penetrative sex is justified only where it is marked by respect for sexual autonomy and the goods achieved in the circumstances surrounding the act and the meaning attached to it. These may be dependent on consent but do not follow inevitably from it (Herring and Madden Dempsey 2010).

Prima Facie Legal Wrong

It is important to note that the original claim by Madden Dempsey and Herring was that a sexual penetration was a prima facie *moral* wrong. We claim here that it can also be regarded as a legal wrong. The point is that not all prima facie moral wrongs are also legal wrongs.

Michelle Madden Dempsey (2013, 11) has suggested that in deciding whether a moral wrong is a legal wrong, we need to consider whether the community can call someone to account for that wrong. So, if a person fails to turn up to an appointment, we might see that as a prima facie moral wrong, but it would not be the kind of wrong that we would (normally) expect someone to account to the community for. Punching someone, by contrast, would be an act for which it would be appropriate to call them to account to the community/state. She relies on Raz (1994, 20), who claims that the law must provide 'the conditions for living an autonomous life [by] [...] protecting and promoting the creation of the environment which makes such a life a possibility'. Applying this, she argues:

> To establish conditions within which we can possibly live in a community with one another as free and equal moral agents, individuals must have the final 'say so' over how others treat their body. The state is justified in protecting and enforcing this bodily jurisdiction, to ensure that no one usurps the jurisdiction of another without her 'say so'.

She argues that this means the law must permit people the legal power, through consent, to determine how their body is treated, but does not require the criminalisation of sex per se.

It is not, in other words, appropriate for the community to see an explanation for a sexual act itself. Only where there is a non-consensual act should the law target that for non-criminalisation. She explains:

> legitimate criminalization (at least when it comes to sex) should be primarily concerned with establishing and enforcing our jurisdiction over how our bodies are treated. This account limits the proper scope of criminalization of sexual offences to cases where one has usurped the 'jurisdictional say so' over another person's body.

This argument does not necessarily lead to the conclusion that a sexual penetration should not be seen as a prima facie wrong. We agree with Madden Dempsey's starting point that we need a set of state governance that allows subjects 'to live together in community as free and equal citizens' and in particular that the law needs to protect a person's right to have 'jurisdictional say so' over their body. However, we think the current legal definition fails to do that. As noted in Chapter 1, the current law of rape is quite simply leaving rape only rarely punished. Only a tiny number of rapes are prosecuted. As the Victims' Commissioner explains, for survivors 'the criminal justice system is bound to fail and, worse still, to do so in a way that re-victimises them' (Molina and Poppleton 2020). While clearly it would not be appropriate for the state to call to account anyone who has had sex, it can appropriately call to account anyone who has had sex about whom a complaint of rape has been made. They can then appropriately be asked to justify their act. A society which informs men that they will need to be prepared to provide a justification for any sexual penetration, sends a powerful message that if a man is unsure if his partner is consenting, he should not proceed, because if called to account he will not be able to demonstrate a justification. Instead, it requires parties to show high regard for each other's sexual autonomy.

We highlight the Istanbul Convention (Council of Europe 2012) which has been ratified by the United Kingdom. Article 4.1 states: 'Parties shall take the necessary legislative and other measures to promote and protect the right for everyone, particularly women, to live free from violence in both the public and the private sphere'. The United Kingdom has ratified this convention. As seen in the introduction to this article, it is failing to comply with this in relation to sexual violence against women. We believe that recognising sexual penetration as a wrong requiring justification will send a powerful message protecting women from violence and better ensure justice when they are raped. The current approach, based on the view that only sexual penetration that has not been consented to is a prima facie wrong, is failing to meet those obligations. Indeed, as already stated, the current law is manifestly failing to meet the obligations under the Istanbul Convention.

It might be noted that seeing a sexual penetration as a prima facie legal wrong is precisely the approach taken in other contexts of offences against the person. If someone puts their finger into someone's ear or eye, that will be seen as a prima facie wrong which requires justification, such as consent (or, as we shall argue shortly, belief in consent).

The correct starting point is, therefore, that there is a duty not to have sex with another person. We do not start with the assumption that sex with any other person is permissible unless they resist or manifest opposition. The duty exists until there is, at least, an expression of consent. That is true both in law and morality. That is what the claim of a prima facie legal wrong captures.

The current law takes the perspective that there is not a general legal duty not to have sex. Rather, the duty only arises where the sex is shown to be non-consensual (Madden Dempsey 2023). However, that is not the best approach for the law to take. Starting with a clear legal duty not to have sex unless one can show consent is a better approach for the law to take as it offers better protection to victims of sexual assault. We accept that in making this claim much turns on how one understands the current position of sexual relations. Given the data we cited in Chapter 1, we think that a clear statement of this legal duty is required to combat the epidemic of sexual assault. In a society in which rape and sexual assault are very rare, then perhaps a different approach could be taken, but that is not where we are.

Consent as a Justification or Lack of Consent as an Element of the Wrong

The above argument is jurisprudential and somewhat technical, but in this section, we discuss its practical impact. Generally, in criminal law, consent can be relevant in one of two ways:

- Model 1: Consent operates as a defence. The act will be unlawful unless the defendant can raise a defence, and the consent of the victim can operate as such a defence.
- Model 2: The lack of consent is part of the definition of the offence. The act is only unlawful if it is proved that there is no consent.

This distinction is fundamental to the conceptual basis of the offence. Under Model 1, consent is transformative in rendering an otherwise unlawful act into a lawful one. In Model 2, lack of consent is transformative in rendering an otherwise lawful act into an unlawful one.

The distinction between these is key for two particular reasons. First, there is a key conceptual issue about what can qualify as consent. Under Model 1, the question is whether there is consent and sufficient consent to do the work required of it: to transform an unlawful act into a lawful act. Under Model 2, the key question is whether there is a lack of consent, such as to do the work required of it: to transform a lawful act into an unlawful act. This is particularly key in a case where there is 'marginal' or 'impaired' or 'weak consent' (see Section 'The Concept of Rich Consent', where we discuss further the difference between weak and rich consent). In such a case, under Model 1, the weak consent will be ineffective to justify, while under Model 2, it may be sufficient to mean the case does not become one of 'no consent' and so there is no offence committed (Herring 2023a).

The second significance relates to the burden of proof. Where the lack of consent is seen as part of the *actus reus*,[5] then the prosecution must prove that the *actus reus* is made out. In other words, the prosecution must prove there was no consent. Where, however, the consent operates as a defence, the burden of proof *can* lie on the defendant. We will return to the question of what that burden is later in Section 'Responsibility, Penetration and Consent'.

We will argue in this book that Model 1 is the correct way to understand rape, although we will go on to argue that what is key is the reasonable belief in consent, rather than consent itself that matters. But before doing that, more needs to be said about why Model 1 is appropriate.

To establish that, we go back to our claim that a sexual penetration is a prima facie wrong. Recall this is the argument that a sexual penetration is an act which requires justification. Without there being a justification, sexual penetration harms the victim, interferes with their bodily integrity, generates risks of further harm and expresses a negative meaning. Those are the acts which fit into Model 1: the wrong is there in the nature of the act, but consent can render it justifiable.

Model 2 is appropriate for acts which are not wrong in themselves but become wrong when done without consent. For example, if a tourist was taking a photograph of a landmark and in taking the picture, given the crowded environment, images of passers-by were captured. We might conclude that no wrong is done in taking such a photograph. However, our view might change if a passer-by, spotting the tourist was about to take the photograph

---

5 A Latin term referring to elements of an offence that relate to the acts of the defendant, including their circumstances and consequences.

said, 'please don't take a picture of me'. Then it would be wrong to do so.[6] The absence of consent has changed an act from permissible to impermissible.

How Consent Justifies?

Just to recap where the argument has got to so far. We have claimed that when D sexually penetrates V, he commits a prima facie legal wrong. That is a wrong that can be justified. In the next section, it will be argued that it is not consent that justifies the penetration, but a reasonable belief in consent. To understand that claim, we need to explain how consent works to justify the prima facie wrong in a sexual penetration (Wall 2015). It does so in the following way.

D requires a justification to proceed to engage in a sexual penetration. In other contexts, a defendant engaging in a prima facie wrong may be able to rely on a range of justifications. These might be that the defendant was acting in self-defence; or was seeking to avoid a great harm; or was protecting others, but none of these seem to apply to a sexual penetration. [7] This is because it is not for D, nor anyone else, to determine whether sex between D and V would be good for V. This is V's decision alone. While in other contexts D may have other reasons to believe that an act will promote V's best interests (for example, D is a doctor offering V a treatment that makes them healthier) in relation to sex D has no reason to think the sex will benefit V, save V's own assessment. Indeed, much misogyny and pornography are premised on a kind attitude that a man is in a good position to know if a woman should have sex: 'she wants it really' or 'she needs a good seeing to'. Quite rightly, such attitudes are utterly unacceptable. D is in no position to determine whether sex would be good for V: that must be V's choice.

In short, then, it is acting in a way that respects and promotes V's sexual autonomy, which is what will justify D's action. In other words, D must acknowledge that it is for V to determine whether sex is right for her and that she alone is in a position to judge that (Herring 2016). From this analysis, we can make several key points.

First, consent operates as an 'exclusionary permission'. It permits D to set aside those reasons against having sex and proceed (Müller 2018). Of course, that does not mean that D has to have sex. D may decide for other reasons

---

6   There could be a criminal offence under the Public Order Act 1986, Section 4A, or the Protection from Harassment Act 1997 (if there is a course of conduct).

7   Save, arguably, in bizarre hypotheticals, for example, that the world will be destroyed unless A penetrates B without consent.

(or indeed for no reasons at all) that despite V's consent he will not proceed. However, the consent allows D to accept V's assessment and engage in the penetration. It is also worth noting that V's consent only operates insofar as D has reasons against engaging in sexual penetration that rest in V's rights. If there are reasons against the penetration that rest on the interests of third parties then, of course, V's consent provides no reasons for setting those aside. For example, if D were married and had obligations to his spouse, V's consent has no reasons against setting them aside (Madden Dempsey 2013).

Second, this explanation does much to teach us about what is sufficient to amount to consent. In short, it will require rich consent, a concept explored below in 'The Concept of Rich Consent'. Clearly, silence cannot be relied on to provide the justification just articulated. Nor can any kind of equivocal 'consent'. In these cases, D would have to conclude that it was not clear what V's sexually autonomous wishes were, and so they could not be relied upon to commit a prima facie wrong. Clearly, it is not enough just for V to have said 'yes': it may be that despite the expression of consent, the circumstances of it mean D cannot rely on it in the way described. For example, if D knows that V is saying 'yes' as a result of pressure or based on a fundamental mistake as to the facts, then D cannot use the 'yes' as an assessment by V that the sex is good for them. That requires D to interrogate the consent offered and take steps to ensure that the consent is of the kind required. This requires D to be able to take V's consent as a rich expression of their autonomy (Wall 2017). We will explore that more in 'The Concept of Rich Consent'.

The third point is that a close reading of the argument above will make it clear that it is a reasonable belief in consent, rather than the fact of consent, which is key to justification. That is a complex and controversial point and needs careful explanation, which we undertake in the next section.

What can Justify the Wrong? Consent or Belief in Consent?

If the reader is with us up to this point, the inevitable question is what can justify the prima facie wrong of a sexual penetration. The most obvious answer is the consent of the victim. We will suggest here that this is not quite right. Rather, it is the reasonable belief in consent that provides the justification.

Madden Dempsey (2013) explains that V's consent gives D an 'exclusionary permission to disregard reasons against acting that are grounded in the well-being of the person who consented'. She explains

> When the exclusionary option is taken up by the person ([D]) whose conduct calls for the other's ([V]'s) consent, the moral quality of [D]'s

conduct is transformed, such that [D]'s conduct no longer constitutes a wrong against [V].

Consent does this work by providing D with a reason (a permission) to set aside reasons against penetration.

Note, however, that the focus under this explanation is on what consent does for the reasons D has for acting; not what consent in the abstract does. It is the taking up by D of those good reasons which justifies the act (Gardner 2010). Marcia Baron (2017) writes:

> [...] when we ask 'Was S justified in doing x?' or claim that she was justified, our attention is as much on S as on x. We are evaluating S's conduct. What matters is how the agent conducted herself. With this in mind we consider not what S should have done had she been omniscient, but whether S acted reasonably. When a belief component is critical, the issue is whether the belief(s) on which her action was based was, or were, reasonable. The issue is not whether the belief was true.

This is particularly key for the law where it is directing to people what reasons that the law may accept as justifying their otherwise criminal behaviour (Grenawalt 1984; Alvarez 2017).

While it is not particularly controversial to suggest an act is only justified if D acts based on reasonable beliefs that are accepted by the law as providing a justification, it is more controversial to claim that whether or not the justifying reasons existed is not legally relevant. To clarify, we are here considering a case where D reasonably believes he is justified in engaging in sexual penetration, but does it matter whether in fact there was consent?

We accept that, at a theoretical level, it might. Jesse Wall (2015, 294) argues:

> If sexual penetration is a wrong, it will only be justified if there are reasons that permit the action ('guiding reasons') and if these were the ones that the defendant acted on ('explanatory reasons'). A person's internal attitude of willingness or acquiescence (his or her 'attitudinal consent') towards the specific act can provide the necessary guiding reasons to justify the wrong. However, words and conduct that manifest or express this internal attitude ('expressive consent') are also needed in order to provide the applicable explanatory reasons to justify the wrong.

As he explains, relying on the work of John Gardner, a justification requires there to in fact be reasons for justifying the acts and that D acted on those reasons.

There are two cases to consider. The first is where V consents, but D does not reasonably believe there is consent. For the reasons given above, D is not justified because D is not acting for justifying reasons. The second is where V does not consent but D reasonably believes she does. Under most models of justification, D will not be able to rely on a mistaken belief as providing a justification. We think that in the context of rape, however, the issue is less clear.

Key to the justification of a sexual penetration is that the defendant is seeking to rely on the consent of the victim as an expression of her full autonomous desire. In other words, the attitude D is expressing towards V's sexual autonomy is crucial. Even if it turns out that V was consenting, if D is not acting for the justifying purpose (seeking to respect V's sexual autonomy), then he cannot be justified.

It is important to note that sexual relations are somewhat unusual in terms of justification. In many other instances where a defendant is seeking to justify a prima facie wrong, there may be a broad range of potential justifications: saving the life of another; preventing damage to property; acting in accordance with a lawful order, and so forth. However, it is hard to imagine a sexual penetration ever being justified in such terms. Only the consent of the victim is a route into a justification. So, here the attitude of the defendant, the core justifying feature, is foundational to consent.

The importance of the defendant's attitude towards the victim's consent is reflected in some of the feminist writing on the wrong of rape. Brownmiller (1975, 376) claims:

> rape is not a crime of irrational, impulsive, uncontrollable lust but [...] a deliberate hostile violent act of degradation and possession [...] designed to intimidate and inspire fear

Du Toit (2009, 88) in her discussion of women's accounts of rape emphasises how it involves 'the violent erasure of a woman victim's sexual subjectivity'. These accounts do not posit the woman's lack of consent per se as the core wrong. The wrong is the male act which ignores, or does not care about, the consent. In theory, the 'degradation and possession' and 'erasure of subjectivity' could be consistent with there being consent. The focus is on the attitude and acts of the man, not the mindset of the victim. As Rose Owen (2024) argues:

> Rape, sex, and pornography as forms of violence transform women into objects through the use of force. Women under the threat of patriarchal violence thus exist as 'living corpses' solely for the satisfaction of men's sexual pleasure. Once we recognize violence as objectification, we see the political harms of violence: namely, that it erases people – in the case of sexual violence, largely women – from shared political life.

Under this understanding as rape being objectifying violence, the consent or otherwise of V is rather beside the point. It is the attitude of D towards V and V's sexual autonomy that is key.

There are different ways of expressing the response to a case where V does not consent but D believes V does. We might focus on the defendant's good reason for acting as he did and rely on those justifying the act; or, more plausibly, say that the defendant is excused from acting as he did because he was not to blame for following the reasonable reasons he did (Gardner 2009). However, it is expressed that it is clear that the defendant is not guilty if he reasonably believes in consent and should have no legal justification if he does not believe in consent. Therefore, the consent of V is irrelevant. The focus of whether sex is justified is whether the defendant had good reasons for acting as he did and whether he acted for those good reasons. To repeat, it is not the consent itself that does any of the moral or legal work of consent, but how D understands and responds to that consent (Healey 2019).

The Concept of Rich Consent

We mentioned above that consent should be understood as richly autonomous consent. We need to explain this concept further. To explain that concept, we emphasise that autonomy is scalar: a decision may be more or less informed; there may be more or less scope for deliberation; there may be more or less pressure, and so forth. By referring to a richly autonomous decision, we mean to indicate that the individual is aware of all the important information and the information they want to know about the issue; they have the time to deliberate and reach a careful decision that reflects their values and identity, and that they are free from outside pressure.

At the two ends of the spectrum of consent, we have rich and weak consent, which we define as follows:

- Consent in a rich sense would require us to be strict about what will count as consent. The person must know all of the relevant facts and be able to weigh them in the balance and reach a decision for themselves. They must be free from illegitimate pressure and feel they have a range of options open to them. Finally, their consent must be a positive enthusiasm to proceed.
- Consent in the weak sense would mean we would not be strict about what would count as consent. The person need only know the essential facts. They need to be able to come to a decision, but we will not have requirements about the quality of their decision-making. Unless they are facing overwhelming pressures, we will accept their consent as valid.

We believe that only rich consent can do the work in justifying sexual penetration. As we discussed in 'How Consent Justifies?', D must be able to say of V, 'She has made the decision to agree to sex and has decided that is what she wants to do. I will accept her assessment as she alone has the right to decide whether she wants to have sex' (Herring 2023). That clearly requires more than the mere saying of 'yes'. Consent should not be seen as a game whereby the object is to get the other party to say 'yes', but rather than attitude of respect towards the other party's sexual autonomy. This means that D must believe that V has made the decision for herself as an expression of her autonomy, informed about the matters that matter to her, with time, space and freedom to deliberate, free from pressures. If D is to have the attitude of respect for autonomy that we have discussed, this means that D has a responsibility to ensure any consent given is full, rich and autonomous.

The difficulty is that in our society, accepting subpar consent as sufficient to amount to consent for the purpose of rape is commonplace. As Suzanne Zaccour (2023) has highlighted 'Regular sexual availability is perceived as essential to the maintenance of an intimate relationship', and this means that women feel pressured to 'satisfy men's fantasies even when they do not desire the sexual activity in question'. She highlights the ways in which behaviour such as 'sulking' or threatening to end a relationship if sex is refused is rarely seen as coercive ways of obtaining 'consent'.

While we might see consent at a theoretical level as operating as a scalar concept, it is, for legal purposes, as Madden Dempsey (2023) puts it, 'a threshold concept, not a matter of degree'. There is either consent or there is not as far as the law is concerned. There is no concept of 'partial consent' or 'mega consent' for that matter. To Madden Dempsey, this means that cases which might be problematic in terms of morality do not cross the threshold for rape. She gives the example of 'B agreeing to sex with A to cheer A up, or out of a sense of duty or guilt, despite B not desiring the sex'. She justifies this on the basis that if the threshold of knowledge, capacity and voluntariness is met, then the consent should be legally justified because people must be given fair warning to know clearly when their consent is legally valid or not. In relation to her example, she explains:

> While it is almost certainly morally wrong, all things considered, to have sex with someone who does not desire it, the state should not use its power to prohibit sex if the undesiring person nonetheless consents to it. It is up to each person to determine when they are willing to have sex, and it is possible to be willing to have unwanted sex.

We find this less straightforward. Madden Dempsey's way of expressing it: that a person should be able to consent to have sex they do not want to have, is not the right question. The question should be whether it is right for D to proceed to have sex with V if he is aware she does not want it. In such a case, D may not have sufficient reason to proceed with the penetration. If D is aware V is 'consenting' as a result of external or internal pressures, this may not be sufficiently rich consent to justify the penetration. This is not to say that D must believe that V is wildly enthusiastic about sex, but D must at least believe there is rich consent.

For a person to be fully autonomous, they must understand the information relevant to the decision. In addition, Jesse Wall (2017) summarises the philosophical literature on autonomy and lists the following three requirements:

(i)   to act free from undue interference or influence of others (the freedom condition);

(ii)   to exercise the capacity for rational thought and cognition (the competence condition); and

(iii) to act according to the beliefs, values and commitments that the person identifies or endorses *as their own* beliefs, values and commitments (the authenticity condition).

These are echoed in Makenzie and Rogers' (2013, 39–40) work, which explores these three key elements of autonomy:

- Self-determining: being 'able to determine one's own beliefs, values, goals and wants, and to make choices regarding matters of practical import to one's life free from undue interference. The obverse of self-determination is determination by other persons, or by external forces or constraints'.

- Self-governing: 'being able to make choices and enact decisions that express, or are consistent with, one's values, beliefs and commitments. Whereas the threats to self-determination are typically external, the threats to self-governance are typically internal, and often involve volitional or cognitive failings. Weakness of will and failures of self-control are common volitional failings that interfere with self-governance'.

- Having authenticity: 'a person's decisions, values, beliefs and commitments must be her 'own' in some relevant sense; that is, she must identify herself with them and they must cohere with her 'practical identity', her sense of who she is and what matters to her. Actions or decisions that a person feels were foisted on her, which do not cohere with her sense of herself, or from which she feels alienated, are not autonomous'.

Where these requirements are not met a person may be expressing a view, but it is not 'their' view. They are not directing their own life or course of action; their decisions are a reflection of the views of others. Consent in cases where these conditions are met tells us more about the circumstances V was in than it does about V's own views.

We explore this further in the next section, which focuses on the importance of vulnerability and relationality when considering consent.

Vulnerability, Relationality and Consent

When the law conceives of what we mean by consent and how we expect those who are not consenting to behave, much depends on the nature of the self that is taken as the standard norm. The law has taken a particular understanding of the self as a liberal legal autonomous subject, one that is assumed to be self-sufficient, capable and free to consent or withhold consent as they so wish. As commentators such as Ngaire Naffine (2020); Natalie Stoljar (2017); Jonathan Herring (2019) and Jennifer Nedelskey (2013) have argued, this is a false image of the self. Consent and the idea of being able to say yes or no is so closely intertwined with this autonomous framing of the legal subject it must be unpacked.

This is obviously central to the problematic framing of the legal subject. But, even more so than that, such a formation of the legal subject is an inaccurate representation of our lived experience (Herring, 2019). It assumes we are independent beings who do not need each other, that we live and exist in a vacuum of self-sufficiency. This does not reflect the reality of our lived experiences and our ontological being. We are not independent and self-sufficient; rather, we are vulnerable and interdependent, both on each other and on the state. By vulnerable, we are not claiming to be so in the negative way in which it has been historically and colloquially understood. Instead, we mean in a way that reflects both our susceptibility to good and bad, and our overall fluid state of being that needs others in order to exist and to flourish.

It is not within the scope of this book to detail how different vulnerability theorists have defined vulnerability (Fineman, 2017). Instead, we will explain some of the main components of a vulnerability theory to help us challenge the current formation of the legal subject as an autonomous one. In doing so, we can help reframe the narrative and start to think about how we can move away from responsibilising victims to avoid harm, and instead shift the spotlight onto the defendants.

Insights from theories of vulnerability have one thing in common; almost all vulnerability scholars agree on our universal vulnerability. What that means is we are all vulnerable to harm by our very nature, because of our fleshiness, because of our mere existence as humans, our embodiment. Whilst this initially might not seem like a radical breakthrough starting point, it does in fact completely undermine the foundations of the current liberal legal autonomous subject. What is the relevance of this discussion of the self to the offence of rape? We highlight three particular points.

First, recognising ourselves as inherently vulnerable highlights the importance of taking care of each other. As Gilson (2014) has gone even further to say, we are not only vulnerable to harm, but vulnerable to change and to good. We can feel the true extent of love when we have suffered a loss, and we can grow to learn when we leave ourselves open to failure. What that means is we can flourish with each other, so long as we respect and support each other to do so. We cannot make decisions in isolation. Our choices impact each other; our actions have a ripple effect beyond our own selves. It follows then that, as a result, we need to be mindful of one another. We have a duty of care to one another, particularly not to exploit each other's vulnerabilities (Herring 2019, ch 7). We have duties to ensure one's vulnerability is respected and acknowledged and given the opportunity to thrive. Indeed, a very apt example of being exposed to the opportunity to thrive or be harmed is that of sexual relationships. There is potential for lust, love, desire, pleasure and intimacy, but also the potential for physical and emotional harm, to exploitation and to degradation. We must therefore be mindful of that vulnerability when considering how to respond in the law. Indeed, in identifying this heightened experience of vulnerability, we become less concerned by the victim's consent and instead ask questions about the defendant and his actions – particularly ensuring he was not relying on myths and stereotypes to support his belief in consent

Second, understanding universal vulnerability means we are sensitive to each other's failings and weaknesses. When we start from a position that assumes we are all capable and free independent rational beings, we assume consent can be easily given or denied, and therefore assume we can easily take responsibility for our own actions and prevent harm being done to us. Indeed, many legal doctrines assume this starting point, such as in contract law, where the principle of 'caveat emptor': Let the buyer beware (Buchanon, 1970). This doctrine presupposes that the purchaser is in a good position to make choices and to determine whether or not they should purchase the goods; they must look out for themselves as it is not up to the seller to highlight any defects. Indeed, if the purchaser fails to identify any issues that are later uncovered, they only have themselves to blame. Arguably, we can draw similarities to that of rape too. When the victim says 'yes', we assume that is consent and the product of a rational, free and informed choice. Something very extreme and overt, such a threat of death or impersonation, is required to persuade us that a person is not acting in an independent rational way. Similarly, where a victim of rape is assumed to be rational, reasonable and capable of protecting themselves, they should do so. They should only have themselves to blame if they act in a provocative way, engage in 'dangerous behaviours', or fail to properly communicate their non-consent to the defendant.

Third, an understanding of the relational self challenges the assumptions about what we expect of victims. Reinforcing notions of rational standard responses can then lead to a 'hierarchy of victimisation' (Gotell, 2008, p 879) and contribute to myths and stereotypical assumptions of what is expected of rape victims, creating the concept of an 'ideal victim' (Daly 2022). Christie (1986) originally described the ideal victim as someone who is traditionally vulnerable, 'defenceless, innocent' and worthy of 'sympathy and compassion', who is a completely blameless, 'security conscious, crime preventing subject' (Gotell, 2008 p. 879). A rational independent woman would not walk home alone at night, intoxicated, alone, wearing a short skirt. Moreover, not even conforming to the real rape script, when we consider acquaintance rapes, these become even harder to prove. Allegations of rape should be timely, with evidence of resistance and no apparent blame to the victim.

However, as the majority of rapes are by acquaintances and not a 'stranger in the bushes', it becomes increasingly difficult for women to conform to the rational ideal victim. Most rapes occur with some level of intoxication, which of course opens up scrutiny of the victim's behaviour and often acts as a distraction from the defendant's behaviour. Likewise, the further the woman deviates from the ideal rational victim, the more exposed she becomes to lines of questioning that inherently support rape myths and stereotypes, which actively undermine her credibility. As we have said elsewhere,

> there is almost a double bind here: if the woman has put herself in a position to be raped it is assumed this is evidence of her independence, autonomy and lack of vulnerability; and those self-same characteristics means she would make utterly manifest her opposition and would respond appropriately by, for example, reporting it to the police. A failure to do so is an indication she must have consented. If she claims that she was too vulnerable to act in this way, this will be disbelieved because she would never have put herself in the position to be raped, if she had not been sufficiently autonomous to do so. (Herring and McCormack 2025)

It is this vulnerability that creates shared responsibilities, both positive and negative ones to one another, which we outline below (see also McCormack and Herring 2024a). Ultimately, we say a defendant should ensure that the woman has time to make a decision free from any undue pressure or persuasion, and a defendant must ensure that her vulnerability is not exploited. Any legislation governing sexual relationships should reflect those responsibilities.

Fourth, a relational understanding of the self recognises that consent is a co-operative enterprise. It is imperative for consent to be able to do the justificatory work it needs to; an individual must be given the utmost opportunity to exercise autonomy. Rather than presupposing individuals are autonomous and therefore ignoring the environmental and situational circumstances in which that apparent consent is expressed, we argue for a recognition of our situational and embodied vulnerability and the need for a rich, full and complete expression of autonomous wishes and desires. We must avoid a situation where a D sees a 'yes' as the end goal and uses tactics to achieve that aim with no real consideration for the genuine wants and needs of V. He must be confident that any consent given is not as a result of societal expectations, pressures or coercion, tricks or taps; rather, it is an authentic expression of her will. This is why the focus on him and his awareness, rather than the existence of consent, can do the groundwork in shifting the focus away from the victim and onto the defendant whilst still respecting the autonomy of the victim.

Consent as a State of Mind or an Outward Expression

We have so far avoided an issue that has been a dominant theme in the literature, and that is whether consent should be understood as something internal to V (V's state of mind) or an external expression (whether V communicated consent). In other words, do we focus on what V said or did, or do we focus on what was in V's mind? Renzo (2022) distinguishes between the 'mental state view' which sees consent as a state of mind and the 'behavioural view' which sees consent as a state of mind that is communicated to the other person.

The debate is often characterised by a reference to the 'affirmative consent model'. This requires that, to amount to consent, there must be an expressed positive desire by V, rather than an approach which says there is consent unless V manifests opposition to it. But there is more to discuss than this. Drawing on Hörnle (2023) we might imagine three different versions of an affirmative consent model:

1. There needs to be positive approval as a mental state; communication is irrelevant.
2. The mental state is irrelevant, but there needs to be communication of positive approval.
3. There needs to be both positive approval as a mental state and a communication of positive approval.

So, under approach 1, the consent question would be entirely focused on V's state of mind. What was said or done by V would be irrelevant save as evidence of their state of mind. For approach 2, the focus would be entirely on the communication. What was in B's mind would be irrelevant. For approach 3, we can see that both the victim's state of mind and the communication from the victim are what matters.

It should be clear from our argument so far that approach 1 is implausible. It is crucial that the law provides clear guidance for people wishing to sexually penetrate another. As Hörnle (2023) has noted, attempting to ascertain the inward thoughts of a person is difficult because 'the existence of a mental state does not necessarily imply the formulation of coherent sentences or, for that matter, the formulation of any sentences at all'. More importantly, she notes, 'mental states are not accessible to others and thus cannot play a crucial role in guiding conduct'. So, focusing on whether a clear consent was expressed is more straightforward than determining what a person's state of mind was. Further, in light of our arguments above, the key role for consent must be as a means of guiding D's behaviour. If the role of V's consent is to change the practical reasoning of D, then it can only do this if it is in a form that is assessable to D. It cannot, therefore, rest in V's mind alone (McCormack and Herring 2024).

That leaves options 2 and 3. It is not normally made clear by supporters of affirmative consent which of these two models they support. We think it must be option 3: that there needs to be positive approval as both a mental state and as communicated. The case which demonstrates this well is *R v. McFall* (1994). There the defendant kidnapped his former partner. The defendant had a gun and forced the victim into a hotel. There he made her take a bath and then have sex with her. The victim at the trial stated she had faked orgasms during the sex; indeed, she said she had done that so well she might have made the defendant believe she was consenting. The Court of Appeal upheld the rape conviction. That must be the right outcome. Although outwardly (in terms of communication) the victim may have been displaying consent, even enthusiasm, it was clear that internally she was strongly objecting to the act. In terms of the *mens rea*, the Court of Appeal took the view that in the circumstances no reasonable jury would conclude the defendant reasonably believed the victim was consenting. It would be absurd to acquit in a case like this where the defendant knew the victim did not genuinely consent and in her mind the victim was not consenting, merely on the basis she had 'performed' consent in a bid to save her life. Of course, where a victim is manifesting consent, but internally is not consenting, it may be that the defendant lacks *mens rea*. But where the defendant has the *mens rea*, there should no barrier to finding there to be no consent based on the fact there was a manifestation of consent, which D knew did not reflect the true situation.

Responsibility, Penetration and Consent

It should be clear that our approach puts considerable weight on the idea that a man who sexually penetrates a woman owes duties of responsibility towards her. This is because he knows that he is about to undertake what is a prima facie harmful act against her, and so he owes duties to ensure that those harms are avoided. In particular, he has a duty to ensure that he has good reason to believe that she is consenting in a rich sense. This, we have argued, is a legal as well as a moral duty. This rests on the fact that the act will be a very serious harm if he has the consent issue wrong.

It should be recalled that no one has any reason to decide for someone else that sex is good for them. Indeed, the mindset that a man can tell if a woman needs sex or that a woman will inevitably benefit from sex with him is precisely the kind portrayed in pornography but is rightly rejected. Ensuring, therefore, that the consent is sufficiently rich to justify consent is key.

This responsibility leads to both negative and positive duties.

Negative duties

As argued above, only belief in a richly autonomous decision by V that she wants to have sex can be relied on as effective consent by D. For D to have that belief, D cannot have sought to interfere in V's decision-making in a way to reach an outcome D wants. The kind of behaviour that would do that includes:

i)   exploitation, including offering inducements;
ii)   deception;
iii) use of force;
iv)   threats of force; and
v)   undue pressure, including threats of emotional harm such as breaking off the relationship; threats to commit self-harm and repeated requests.

Where D acts in these ways that indicate that D is not seeking to allow V to make V's own assessment of whether they want to have sex, but rather D is trying to get V to express what D wants to hear: 'consent' to sex in our context.

Positive duties

If D is genuinely trying to determine whether or not V has offered full rich consent, it may not be enough simply to avoid interference in V's decision-making.

Where someone is aware that their actions risk causing avoidable serious harm to another, they have a legal responsibility to take steps to ensure they do not act in a way that harms the other (Goodin, 1985; Collins, 2013). D must therefore listen carefully to V and appreciate how V understands the act within its wider relational and social meaning (Herring, 2009). D should be seeking to do what he reasonably can to enable V to make a free, informed decision about sex. That might require positive steps, such as the provision of information, the removal of sources of pressure or giving time to make the decision (McCormack and Herring 2024).

The Need for Reasonable Belief

So far we have established that D's penetration is a prima facie wrong. For D to be justified in that penetration, he must reasonably believe that V consented, understood in a rich sense, to the penetration. In this section, we explain why the belief in consent must be reasonable; it being insufficient for there to be simply an honest belief.

The starting point is that, as already established, the act of sexual penetration is a prima facie wrong. It therefore requires the defendant to exercise 'due diligence' in ensuring that there are reasonable grounds for the belief (Dougherty 2021; Wall 2019). D must be aware that if he gets the consent question wrong, then he will be doing serious harm to V. In other words, D must be aware that he is about to engage in an act that is endangering V. This puts an obligation on him to ensure that he has the consent question correct. We highlight three particular reasons why it is, therefore, appropriate to require a reasonable belief in consent.

First, the risks associated with sex are well known. It is unlikely anyone embarking on a sexual interaction will be unaware of the importance of getting consent. As D is aware that they are about to perform an act which could cause serious harm, they are put on notice that they should make sure they have consent.

Second, it is very easy for D to acquire reasonable grounds for their belief in consent. In many cases, it will be sufficient to simply ask or ensure that V is indeed consenting. If there is a question about V's knowledge, then D can, if he wishes to proceed, disclose that knowledge.

Third, if D is uncertain about whether there is consent, then there is a simple course of action available: simply not proceeding with the sexual interaction. This is hardly an onerous imposition on D. This makes rape different from other crimes, such as criminal damage or battery, where avoiding ever risking touching someone or damaging property would require you to stay in bed all day!

We accept there is some room for debate around the idea of a reasonable belief. To what extent is there to be an element of subjectivity? Is the question whether it was reasonable for D to believe there was consent, or whether the reasons themselves were objectively good reasons to act on the belief (Gardner 1991). In other words, to what extent can we say it was reasonable for him (as a pornography addict or a committed INCEL believer) to believe there was consent; or is the question whether, objectively assessed, the consent was justified? Our proposal recommends a purely objective test, which would hold the actions of the D to the standards of a reasonable juror. If we take a purely objective approach to assessing the reasonableness of the belief in consent, we could achieve two things. Firstly, we would be holding all defendants to an expected standard of behaviour, which acknowledges the prima facie wrongfulness of penetration and the need for their actions to be justified. In determining whether the belief in consent was justified, the legislation could make reference to the positive and negative duties as outlined above. Moreover, this could place further onus on the D, therefore further scrutinising their behaviour. This objective standard of expected behaviour may in turn help to prevent D from relying on, or allowing them the opportunity to use, a narrative informed by stereotypes and myths to justify their actions. As the issues around consent and sex are well known, it does not seem unreasonable to expect the pornography addict, for example, to say 'I should be aware my views around sex are impacted by my pornography use and so I should be particularly careful to ensure there is consent' or the public school boy to say 'I have not have had much experience of interacting with women and so I must make absolutely sure I have correctly understood what she wants'. We repeat Connaghan's (2019, 182) call that rape should set 'what kinds of socio-sexual relations we are trying to promote or discourage'. These are that people should take care in their sexual interactions. In the examples above, D will be aware that, for example, due to their schooling, they lack familiarity with women and/or that their pornography use has impacted on their attitude towards consent, and so they need particular care to ensure they have consent. The problem of sexual stereotypes in relation to consent is well known and again seems to require men to take extra special care to ensure they are not seeking to use a stereotype as a justification for the sex.

Allowing a subjective test for *mens rea* (e.g. that the defendant is guilty unless he honestly believes in consent) allows the defendant to rely on rape myths to justify his beliefs (see the discussion in Chapter 3). As Elinor Mason (2021) notes, cases where D unreasonably believes that V is consenting nearly always rely on sexist ideology and/or some form of rape myth. She argues, 'The law should give fair warning that the offence of rape does not recognize internalized sexist ideology as an excusing condition'. This, the law can clearly do by requiring that the defendant's belief in consent is reasonable.

Burden of Proof and Belief

Having established that D must have reasonable grounds for his belief, we then turn to the issue of burden of proof. As D has committed a prima facie legal wrong, it is appropriate to require D to justify the wrong. There are four options here.

1. That the prosecution must prove that D lacked a reasonable belief.
2. That D carries an evidential burden. In other words, D must introduce evidence that at least raises an issue that he had a reasonable belief in consent.
3. That D carries the burden of proving on the balance of probabilities that D had a reasonable belief in consent. If D is able to satisfy the jury of this, he has a defence and is not guilty. If he cannot show the jury that, on the balance of probabilities, he had a reasonable belief in consent, he will be guilty.
4. That D must prove beyond reasonable doubt that he has a reasonable belief in consent.

The fourth option appears hard to justify. There are no examples in criminal law where there is such a burden on the defendant. We therefore focus on the first three options, all of which have examples in criminal law. To raise the defence of insanity, the defendant needs to prove the defence on the balance of probabilities in line with Model 3. Model 2 reflects the way the rebuttable presumptions work under Section 75 of the Sexual Offences Act 2003 (see Chapter 2, Section 'The Confusing Law on Consent'). The defence of self-defence, in theory at least, falls under Model 1, with the prosecution bearing the burden of showing the defence did not exist.

The law on burdens of proof is complex, and it is not possible to undertake a full analysis here. To some, it is improper in a criminal trial to ever put a burden of proof on a defendant because of the presumption of innocence. That view would suggest Model 1 should be followed. However, a more popular opinion is that the presumption of innocence means that the core elements of the offence must be proved by the prosecution; it is legitimate to put some kind of burden of proof on a defendant in relation to defences (Hamer 2007) than for elements of the core offence (Duff 2005). If this latter view is taken, then Model 2 or 3 can be justified.

We believe Models 2 or 3 are appropriate for two reasons. First, as argued above, we suggest that the core wrong of rape is the sexual penetration and that D needs to justify their actions. This requires them to show that they were acting based on a reasonable belief that V consented in a rich way. Two of the key arguments behind our approach are that D should only proceed with having sex if he is confident that V has provided rich consent and that he can justify his belief, and that the focus of the trial should be on the defendant and whether he had reasonable grounds for his belief. By requiring him to introduce evidence of the reasonableness of his belief under either Model 2 or 3 is services that end. Secondly, the evidence for the justifying belief is evidence to which D will have unique access. The prosecution is in a difficult position to establish what he was thinking and why at the time of the penetration. It is not overly burdensome to expect him to produce evidence of that.

Between the second and third options, there is more to debate. The starting point may be to emphasise the presumption of innocence and the general reluctance in criminal law to use a 'reverse burden of proof': where the defendant must establish evidence to prove an element of the crime. It might be argued that we should depart from that principle to the minimum extent possible, and therefore Model 2 should be preferred. Notably, in the case of the evidential presumptions in the Sexual Offences Act, Model 2 was supported.

The presumption of innocence argument should not be overstated. In *Salabiaku v. France* (1988), the Eureopan Court of Human Rights confirmed that a reverse burden was compatible with the presumption of innocence if a Contracting State uses a reverse burden 'within reasonable limits which take into account the importance of what is at stake and maintain the rights of the defence'. When the courts discuss whether a reverse burden can be appropriate, the following factors have been considered:

- the seriousness of the crime (*R v. Lambert* 2001)
- whether the fact subject to the reversal is part of the core of the offence (*R v. DPP, Ex p Kebilene* 2000)
- when the particular crime is a regulatory offence of which the defendant had notice had had chosen to perform (*R v. Johnstone* 2003)
- the ease of proving the fact in question (*Attorney General's Reference No 4 of 2002* 2004)

Those seeking to promote Model 2 are likely to highlight the gravity of offence and the importance of the presumption of innocence. Those promoting Model 3 are likely to note the ease for a defendant in proving their belief and the importance society attaches to protecting sexual autonomy. On balance, this book promotes Model 2.[8]

---

8 Although one of (JH) is more drawn to Model 3.

Chapter 5

PUTTING THE LAW INTO PRACTICE

A Proposal for the New Law

Bringing these thoughts together, we are in a position to set our proposed definition of rape. Remember, the current definition, found in Section 1 of the Sexual Offences Act 2003, states the *actus reus* of rape is the penile penetration of another without their consent. It places the victim's consent at the heart of the definition of the wrong. By contrast our proposal is as follows:

> D is guilty of rape if he sexually penetrates V without a reasonable (objectively assessed) belief in V's consent (richly understood).

Notably, under this proposal, whether V consents or not is irrelevant. Nothing beyond the penetration is required to show the act is a legal wrong. In a case where the victim is silent or equivocal, the wrong of rape is made out. That is because it does not need to be shown positively that there was opposition (*R v. Malone* [1998]). The defendant will be criminally liable for the penetration unless he can raise a defence/justification by demonstrating the act was justified by his attitude towards the victim, manifested by a reasonable belief in consent, understood as a rich expression of autonomy (see Chapter 4, Section 'The Concept of Rich Consent').

This formulation reflects our claim that a sexual penetration is a prima facie legal wrong. That a penile penetration needs to be justified for it to be lawful. We have explained that the justification comes through the defendant's respect of the victim's sexual autonomy, by taking reasonable steps to ascertain whether the penetration was what she richly autonomously wanted. This justification can come through the execution of duties by the defendant, both positive and negative ones, so that the defendant has reasonable grounds to believe in consent.

We have sought in previous chapters to set out the theoretical arguments for our approach, but we are primarily driven towards our proposal by the practical benefits. First, as mentioned in Chapter 3, the current law leads to an over-scrutiny on the victim's behaviour in the court room. This leads to narratives where the victim's character and testimony is subject to intense scrutiny, informed by stereotypes and myths. The slightest perceived flaw in the victim's evidence or character is magnified by the defence to claim there must be a reasonable doubt. This all leaves the defendant's behaviour underexamined. We seek to refocus the attention of the law on the defendant's behaviour: what he did; what reasons he had for acting in the way he did; and what attitude he was expressing towards the victim.

Second, we believe that our approach enables the law to send a clear and helpful message. Those wishing to engage in sexual penetration should be aware that what they are doing is a prima facie wrong and carries a serious risk of a major harm. They should only proceed if they are confident that their partner has given rich consent. If they are unsure, or their partner appears reticent, or their partner's apparent consent is given in circumstances in which it may not be a rich expression of autonomy (e.g. it is given while experiencing fear or on the basis of a mistake), they should not proceed. If prosecuted, they will need to produce sufficiently strong evidence that they had good reason to proceed with the penetration. Under the current law, the message sent is 'a defendant who sexually penetrates another can only be guilty of rape if it is clear beyond reasonable doubt there is no consent'. Under the proposal, it will be 'a defendant who sexually penetrates another will be guilty of rape unless it is clear that the defendant reasonably believed that the complainant richly consented'. We believe the second message is the correct one to send; it is in line with most teaching in schools and colleges on consent; and best protects women's sexual integrity. This message emphasises the duties that we owe to each other not to cause harm. This acknowledges our vulnerable and relational identities (see Chapter 4, Section 'Vulnerability, Relationality and Consent').

This shift in focus onto the attitude D is expressing towards V's sexual autonomy is a major shift in responsibilities. The focus at the trial would be on D: Did D know what he was doing was wrong? Was D acting for good reason? Did D take steps to ensure he was fully respecting V's sexual autonomy? Did D use any tactics to attempt to manipulate/sway the attitude of the V, so he could feel apparently justified in the penetration? The focus would only be on D's beliefs at the time of the sex. V's post-rape behaviour will be irrelevant because it will tell us nothing about whether the defendant had good reasons to think the victim consented to the sexual interaction. Similarly, V's sexual history or communications with others will be irrelevant unless they were known to D at the time. In focusing on the subjectiveness of the D's belief, we would encourage an in-depth scrutiny of the thoughts and actions of the D to determine whether they truly believed they were permitted to engage in penetration.

Affirmative Consent

As we have already indicated, there is a lively debate over what counts as consent in the law, and whether or not that consent needs to be outwardly expressed (McCormack and Herring 2024b). There have been several campaigns seeking a clear statement in the law that consent to penetration, and indeed any sexual touching, needs to be explicit and clear consent (Right to Equality 2024; Affirmative Consent 2024). 'Only yes means yes' is the popular slogan, aimed to capture this claim. Such campaigns seek to make it clear that a defendant should not rely on an assumption of consent from behaviour, appearance or comments, which do not involve an explicit agreement to have sex. This prevents the defendant claiming that an agreement to 'come to my room for a cup of coffee' is an agreement to have sex; or that dressing in a particular way is an invitation for sexual activity. The concept of affirmative consent becomes clearer when one considers the opposite: that rape only occurs where the victim has made their opposition to a sexual advance clear. This is sometimes called 'resistance rape law' (McCormack and Herring 2024).

English Law has, to a large extent, accepted affirmative consent as a broad principle, although, as we shall see, there are ambiguities around what the concept means. In *R v. Malone* (1998), the Court of Appeal was clear:

> The actus reus of rape is an act of sexual intercourse with a woman who at the time of the act of sexual intercourse does not consent to that act of sexual intercourse. There is no requirement that the absence of consent has to be demonstrated or that it has to be communicated to the defendant for the actus reus of rape to exist.

This is reflected in the language of Section 74 of the Sexual Offences Act 2003: '[...] a person consents if he agrees by choice, and has the freedom and capacity to make that choice'. However, that is not an explicit acceptance of an affirmative consent model. The use of the word 'agreement' could be interpreted to mean that, but it is not beyond debate. While clearly stating that opposition does not need to be manifested in order for there to be a rape conviction, it does not explicitly state that there is rape unless there is explicit consent.

We suggest four primary arguments in favour or the affirmative consent model.

'Freezing'

There is substantial evidence that victims facing a sexual assault 'freeze'. This may be a psychological response to the terror of the attack (Rape Crisis 2024).

It may even be a rational or instinctive realisation that resistance is futile or dangerous. This makes it particularly dangerous to require positive resistance to establish a rape conviction.

The burden on the victim

The resistance rape model places the responsibility on the victim to manifest her opposition. In other words, there is a presumption that any woman consents to sex with any man unless she manifests her opposition. That seems hard to accept and indeed even countries which have a 'resistance rape' law have a requirement that the victim has a reasonable opportunity to resist (Hörnle 2023). Nevertheless, as a matter of principle, it seems wrong to presume consent from any woman to a sexual touching from any man.

It combats rape myths

There is plenty of evidence that men assume that friendliness from a woman or the fact she wears certain clothes amounts to consent (Humphreys and Brousseau 2010). The 'rape resistance' model leaves plenty of scope for the use of such myths (Law Commission 2023). Prohibiting the use of reliance on such assumptions and requiring an explicit consent helps combat these. It also makes it clear the responsibilities the defendant has towards the victim.

Consent justifying a prima facie wrong

If the arguments we have made in Chapter 4 are accepted, then it becomes clear that consent must be a manifest agreement. If there is an ambiguity then quite clearly, the defendant cannot justify his prima facie wrong of the penetration. As argued above, only clear rich consent can offer that.

While these make a strong case for being broadly in favour of an affirmative consent model, care must be taken in expressing how it will work in practice. It would be wrong to simply claim that 'yes means yes'. That could be both over and under-inclusive. It could be under-inclusive because it must be asked whether only the word 'yes' will do or whether words or actions could suffice. It would be odd to require use of a particular word to express consent, not least because the partners may speak different languages. Clearly, what is required are words that are sufficiently ambiguous to indicate positive consent. Similarly, it might be arguable that actions could convey consent. While often actions will be in their nature ambiguous, it seems plausible they could indicate consent, although rarely. If nothing else, sign language could be used by a deaf couple, presumably, to communicate consent. Certainly, between strangers it might be thought that any act will have a degree of ambiguity. Even if, for example, A suggests sex and B undresses and lies on the bed, it might not be quite clear what sexual acts B is consenting to. We might conclude that it would be very rare for anything other than explicit oral communication to communicate unequivocal consent, it cannot be ruled out. Critics might suggest that such an approach is paternalistic, awkward and onerous contract that 'kills the mood'. We would question whether checking for consent ever would kill the mood, but even if this fear is legitimate there is a clear balance. It is better to have a law which occasionally 'kills the mood' than to have a law which fails to protect sexual autonomy. Consent should be ongoing and communicative throughout a sexual encounter. It should be expressed and communicated, usually, but not necessarily, by words.

The second problem with a very simplistic 'yes means yes' model is that sometimes the word 'yes' does not represent true consent. It may be given under threats; based on a mistake or in a state of intoxication and so, as argued in Chapter 4, Section 'The Concept of Rich Consent' fail to constitute 'rich consent'.

Intoxicated Consent

It will be recalled that we are requiring rich consent, by which means it is sufficient to determine that this is a fully autonomous decision by the victim which justifies the defendant in engaging in what would otherwise be a prima facie wrong. It is highly unlikely that an intoxicated consent will be sufficiently clear and rich to justify a prima facie wrongful act. To clarify, by 'intoxicated' we mean more than that a person has had an alcoholic drink, but that the alcohol or drugs have had a marked effect on the person's self-control and/or rationality. Almost in its nature, an intoxicated consent will be insufficient for D to rely on to do an act which could cause such a serious harm.

This is another area where the prima facie wrongfulness of penetration is important. If an act is one which is beneficial to an intoxicated V; for example, D is going to walk V home to a place of safety and warmth; or D is going to make sure that V is sleeping in a way which minimises the dangers of suffocation; then such acts are for V's benefit. In such a case, consent is playing a less important role in justifying what D is doing. Indeed, if V in this case lacks capacity, then under the general principle that in such a case, D can act in way which benefits V. It seems reasonable in the examples above that, generally, D could take it that V would consent to D treating her in a way which promotes her welfare, if V had capacity to do so. However, it is very different where the act is itself a prima facie wrong. Here the consent is justifying an otherwise wrongful act. That is why a rich consent is required. While it is possible for D to reasonably believe that V is giving rich consent, even though V is intoxicated, that will take some evidence. It is most plausible where D and V are long-term partners in a non-abusive relationship.

Consent and Pressure

If V consents under pressure then, if D is aware of that, D cannot take that to be a clear and rich expression of autonomy. D cannot know in such a case whether V has been motivated by the pressure or motivated by a genuine desire to engage in sex.

It is common for academics writing on this issue to explore what kinds of threats will negate consent. For example, should the law only recognise a threat of death or serious harm as negating consent. Wisely English and Welsh law has rejected such an argument.

In *R v. Olugboja* (1982), where the victim was so terrified of the defendant's behaviour that when he approached her, she voiced no resistance to the sex. In upholding the conviction of the defendant, three points stand out. First, she offered no resistance, but she did not offer positive consent.[1] Second, the court rejected any test based on the gravity of the threat to the reasonable person. Rather the question was whether the victim was so terrified that she was unable to give effective consent (Leahy 2014). That means that the nature of the threat was not important, what mattered was the impact of the pressure on the victim. Third, it should be noted that in this case the defendant did not himself utter a threat. He was simply aware that the victim was unable to give free consent. The defendant knew this.

That last point was key in the decision in *R v. Kirk* (2008), where a 14-year-old girl who had previously suffered sexual abuse had run away from home and sleeping on the streets. As the Court of Appeal put it, 'She was tired, dirty and hungry and had nowhere to go' (para 85). She went to see Kirk and asked for money. He offered her £3.25 if she agreed to have sex. She agreed. The prosecution case was she submitted, rather than consented to sex, due to the desperation she felt due to hunger. The Court of Appeal upheld the rape conviction, we believe correctly. The decision rightly acknowledges that the defendant knew that the victim was not in a position to give a richly autonomous consent. It does not matter whether or not the cause of the pressure was from the defendant or an outside source. What was key was that the victim was not able to exercise their sexual autonomy in the way which would justify the defendant engaging in a prima facially wrong way.

---

1 In the case itself, the Court of Appeal saw consent as a state of mind, but drew a distinction between 'real consent' and 'mere submission'.

Consent and Exploitation

There are cases where the victim has said 'yes' and even given the communication of consent, but this was as a result of exploitation. In a sensitive and insightful decision, the Court of Appeal in *R v. Ali* (2015, para 58) recognised how grooming can impact on a person's capacity to express their wishes:

> Although [...] grooming does not necessarily vitiate consent, it starkly raises the possibility that a vulnerable or immature individual may have been placed in a position in which he or she is led merely to acquiesce rather than to give proper or real consent. One of the consequences of grooming is that it has a tendency to limit or subvert the alleged victim's capacity to make free decisions, and it creates the risk that he or she simply submitted because of the environment of dependency created by those responsible for treating the alleged victim in this way. Indeed, the individual may have been manipulated to the extent that he or she is unaware of, or confused about, the distinction between acquiescence and genuine agreement at the time the incident occurred.

As that discussion shows, it is necessary to understand consent in a holistic way, including the relational context within which the decision was made (Dowds 2020). The writing on relational autonomy is helpful here (Makenzie and Rogers 2013; Herring 2009). As discussed in Chapter 4, Section 'Vulnerability, Relationality and Consent', we are relational beings and hence our decisions are made with and through others. However, this means our relationships are both necessary to being autonomous, but can also be a threat to it. It is only by understanding the relational context between the parties that we can understand the extent to which the relationship enabled a richly autonomous decision or whether the decision was the result of exploitation.

In *Ali*, where the context of a grooming relationship demonstrated that while at the time of the sexual acts, there was apparent consent, the relational context revealed that was not so. An even more common scenario will be relationships of domestic abuse in which there may be apparent consent, but that is given while the victim is fearful of violence or emotional abuse if they do not consent. As Catherine MacKinnon (2016) argues:

> The problem with consent-only approaches to criminal law reform is that sex, under conditions of inequality, can look consensual when it is not wanted, at the time because women know that sex that women want is the sex men want from women. Men in positions of power over women can thus secure sex that looks, even is, consensual without that sex ever being freely chosen, far less desired.

This may not be limited to relationships which manifestly fall within coercive control. A study by the NSPCC found that 44 per cent of teenage girls felt guilty if they said no to a request for sex from their boyfriends. Of those who had had unwanted sex with a boyfriend, 55 per cent thought it was partly their fault (BBC 2005). There is now extensive evidence on the pressures on teenage girls to provide sexual images and engage in sexual acts, with these being seen as a normal expectation for a 'good girlfriend' (NSPCC 2024). As Zaccour (2023) has argued, once one starts to unpick the assumptions surrounding heterosexual relationships and the social status they can provide, it becomes harder and harder to find rich consent in opposite-sex relationships. The expectations in opposite sex relationships are that women will Z 'met the sexual needs' or their partners and women may fear negative social and economic consequences if the relationship ends. Zaccour argues that there is within opposite-sex relationships far higher rates of non-consent than have been assumed. As Robin Morgan (1977, 165) writes:

> (T)he pressure is there, and it need not be a knife blade against the throat, it's in his body language, his threat of sulking, his clenched or trembling hand, his self-deprecating humour or angry put-down or silent self pity at being rejected. How many millions of times have women had sex 'willingly' with men they did not want to have sex with?

This highlights the importance on D ensuring that he meets the positive duties towards V in ensuring V has the space and freedom to make a genuine choice and that if D is unsure if there is full consent not to proceed.

Consent and Mistake

A significant amount of literature has addressed the issue of where a victim has appeared to provide consent, but done so on the basis of a mistake. Examples range from a victim consenting to sex, believing her partner is unmarried; or is infertile; or is male. Generally, the issue is presented as asking: What kinds of mistakes are sufficient to 'negate' the consent of the victim? There is surprising consensus as to the broad reply to that: trivial mistakes do not; fundamental mistakes do. The disagreement begins when we must determine who gets to decide which mistakes are fundamental and which are trivial.

Before getting on to that we need to draw some key distinctions. The first is between cases of conditional consent and cases of mistaken consent. An example of the former would be a victim who says: 'I agree to sex as long as you wear a condom', when the defendant does not wear a condom. An example of the second would be a defendant who tells the victim he has had a vasectomy, when he has not, and the victim as a result agrees to sex. We see these as distinct (although closely related). We will justify this distinction in Section 'Conditional Consent'. In this section, we will deal with cases where consent was given to the sexual act, although that consent used a false fact as a basis for deciding to consent. On our approach, there is no substantial difference in the outcome which rests on that distinction, but we discuss it here as it is a theoretical distinction we think is important.

The second key distinction is between a case where the defendant has deceived the victim into believing the false fact and where the victim believes the false fact, but not as a result of a specific statement of the defendant. Again, on our approach, nothing rests on this distinction, but it is one some commentators have placed weight upon. We agree it is a relevant piece of evidence in relation to *mens rea:* it is more plausible that the defendant believed in the victims consent where there is no fraud. However, we see consent as primarily a matter of the victim's state of mind and the expression of that state of mind. If the victim is mistaken as to a key fact, no difference turns on whether this is a result of a false statement from the defendant or for any other reason.

Our proposed response to cases of mistaken consent should be apparent from the arguments made above. If D knows, or ought to know, that V has consented based on a mistaken belief which would have led them not to consent, then D cannot claim to be respecting V's sexual autonomy and using V's consent in the permitted way we described above. If D knows that had V known the truth, she would not be consenting to sex with him, then D can hardly claim to be respecting V's choice regarding sexual matters (Herring 2005). Of course, if V is mistaken about something that D reasonably believes V would not care about, that would not defeat D's reasonable belief defence.

Our proposal then is that if D knows, or ought to know, that V is mistaken as to a 'key fact' and had V known of that 'key fact', V would not have consented, then D cannot rely on V's apparent 'consent'. Note that D may think that V is foolish, petty or even bigoted in placing such weight on such a fact. Indeed, it may even be that most people would think that V is being foolish, petty or even bigoted, but that is beside the point. It is for V to decide what is important for them about sex. That is the whole idea about sexual autonomy. People get to decide for themselves with whom and when they want to have sex. If V does not want to have sex with people who are married to others; who have not said their prayers; or who has blond hair, they are entitled to make that decision, however bizarre that may be others. If D is to have the justifying attitude of respect to V's sexual autonomy, D must respect that. If D knows that V would not have consented, because D has not said his prayers; if D proceeds with sex, he is imposing his own view of what is important about sex on V. He is not showing respect for her decision. D should not be relying on his own assessment of what is important about sex, but respecting the assessment of his partner.

This is not the approach taken by the English and Welsh courts, and by most commentators. Instead the preference is for the law to determine what counts as fundamental issue and only accept that consent is negated when the mistake relates to a matter which is seen by the law or judges as fundamental. The English courts, following such an approach, have suggested that the only kind of mistakes which should negate consent are those which go to the physical nature of the act. In other words, the victim must be mistaken to a matter 'closely connected to the nature or purpose of sexual intercourse rather than the broad circumstances surrounding it that it is capable of negating consent' (*Lawrance* 2020, para 35). The mistake must relate to the 'physical performance of the sexual act' rather than the 'risks or consequences associated with it' (para 37). In *Lawrance* itself, this meant that even though the defendant declared that he had had a vasectomy and so was infertile, and the victim made it clear she was consenting to sex on that basis, there was no rape because the lie about fertility did not impact on the physical nature of the act. This approach is in line with *R (Monica) v. DPP* (2018), where an undercover police officer infiltrated a group of environmentalist activists. As part of his cover, he entered a relationship with one of the women in the group. They had sexual relations and had children together. Clearly, she would not have agreed to the sex had she known the truth. She believed he was a fellow environmentalist who was in a committed relationship with her. However, her mistake did not relate to the physical nature of the act, which was exactly of the kind she was agreeing to, and so she was found to have consented to the sexual relations and the man was not guilty of rape.

This kind of approach is, we believe, mistaken. We highlight three particular flaws with it. The first is that when asking whether there was consent, we need to ask what it is that V is consenting to. To take an obvious example, being kissed is not consent to penile penetration. Consent to 'sex' does not mean consent to all kinds of 'sex'. Inevitably, the victim when consenting will be consenting to sex understood in a particular way: with a particular person or kind of person; in a particular place; in a particular context and so forth. So D needs to know how V understood the act to determine what it was they were consenting to. The error the courts seem to be making is that consent to sex is seen as consent to a particular physical kind of act. That may be how V understood what it was she was agreeing to, but it may well not. This point is well-captured by Martha Nussbaum (2017, 1) who recalls, 'I certainly intended to consent to intercourse. What I did not consent to was the gruesome, violent, and painful assault that he substituted for intercourse'.

What is often missed is that if emphasising consent is about respecting B's sexual autonomy, then A can only do the act to B, *as B understands that act.* If, for example, B's religious beliefs mean that she will be committing a terrible sin to have sex with A who is married, but the act will be approved of by God if A is not married, then *to her* these two acts are fundamentally different. At least as much, maybe more so, as a kiss is different from intercourse to many other people. There may be plenty of people for whom the marital status of their would-be partner is irrelevant, but that is back to the point earlier: we should be asking what it is B is consenting to, *as she understands it.*

Second, any suggestion that the law might say to V that although to her a particular fact was crucial to consenting is to be regarded as trivial by the law, is deeply misguided. It is not for the law to assess what V thought was important about sex and determine whether this is a valid or genuine matter to regard as fundamental. To take such a line is to suggest that V must provide good or acceptable reasons for why she would not want to have sex with D. But V should be under no obligation to provide acceptable reasons for why she does not want to have sex with D. V does not need to justify not giving D access to her body. The bizarre thing is that the law fully recognises that when it comes to property. If D lies about something, intending to acquire property from V, that will be an offence under the Fraud Act 2006. Under that legislation, it is no defence for D to argue that the matter they lied about was trivial. Why is it we take a strong line against those who use lies to get property, but not those who lie to get sex? (Madhloom, 2019).

Third, we need to recognise as a society that there is a wide diversity of views about the nature and values around sex. These reflect cultural, religious and personal values. It is not for the law to state that one set of reasons not to have sex are significant but another set of reasons are trivial. To do this imposes a particular moral perspective on the world. In particular, at least insofar as the decisions of the English courts, that has been a particular secular Western perspective of sex. It shows an utter lack of respect for cultural and religious diversity that under the current law the issues that concern people around sex which do not relate to the physical act are dismissed as being trivial (Herring 2023).

A further point is that if we do not rely on V's assessment of what is important to them about sex, we have judges or others setting down what they think is important. For example, *in R (Monica) v. DPP* (2018) Lord Burnett explaining *R v. McNally*, (2014), stated: 'As a matter of common sense, there was all the difference in the world between sexual activity with a boy and similar activity with a girl'. That may be his personal opinion, but there are plenty of people who would not see all the difference in the world between sex with a boy and with a girl. This dicta illustrates the problems once we depart from asking what was important to V about the sexual act and ask judges to determine what they think is important about sex.

The points just made are obvious when applied in other contexts. If D is cooking V a meal and V has said they are vegetarian, then most people would agree it would be a morally and legally wrong for C to use meat (if she has the necessary *mens rea*).[2] D might try and raise arguments that vegetarianism is foolishness or that the majority of people would not see eating meat products as a big deal, but that is beside the points. It is V's decision that she does not want to eat meat and D should respect that. D may try and say 'but V agreed to eat a meal', but D knew that to V there was a major difference between eating meat and eating plant-based products. D was failing to respect V's autonomy. It is the same in sex, V's consent must be understood in terms of the act as they understood it and with respect for the matters they regarded as important.

Conditional Consent

As mentioned in the Section 'Consent and Mistake', we regard cases of conditional consent as different from cases of mistaken consent. The fundamental difference is this. In a case of conditional consent, the claim is that the act was not covered by the consent. In cases of mistaken consent, the consent appeared to cover the act, but provided while under a mistake as to the circumstances, and had V known the truth the consent would not have provided. Take for example, *Assange v. Swedish Prosecution Authority* (2011), it was held that if a woman agrees to sex, but only if the man wears a condom, she will not be held to have consented if the man does not wear a condom. In this case, the victim was saying, 'I consent to sex if you wear a condom. I do not consent to sex if you do not wear a condom'. If D goes ahead without a condom, it is clear that there is no consent to act. V had made clear what was consented to and what was not, and D did a non-consented act. This is slightly different to cases where there was consent to the act, but that was based on a mistake (Dougherty 2021).

This means that in a case of conditional consent case, there should be no debate about the nature of the condition (whether it was trivial, etc). It is simply a matter of whether the condition was satisfied. In a case of

---

2 It could be a poisoning offence under Sections 23 or 24 of the Offences Against the Person Act 1861.

mistaken consent then there is a potential argument over whether the mistake is related to a sufficiently serious matter (Alencar 2021). Although, as argued above, we believe that if the mistake related to a matter which was a 'deal breaker' (Doughtery 2021) for V, that is enough to mean there was no consent.

Chapter 6

RESPONDING TO CONCERNS

In this chapter, we will consider some of the potential concerns that people may have with our proposal. To recap, our proposal is to redefine rape so that it has two elements:

1. D has sexually penetrated V.
2. D did not reasonably believe that V consented to the penetration.

It will also be recalled that we understand consent in the above formulation to refer to what we have called rich consent: a full expression of V's autonomy. We have sought to justify this proposal above, we now turn to potential objections.

Symbolic Paternalism

A major concern may be that the proposal is expressing paternalism towards the victim. This objection may be expressed in this way. Our proposal is saying to the victim 'your consent is irrelevant to us'. It is, in other words, yet another example of women being silenced.

We reject this claim for two reasons. The first is that the current law, while purporting to pay attention to women's voices by focusing on the consent of the victim, in fact does the opposite. As described above (Chapter 3, Section 'Cross-Examination'), a range of rape myths; misleading forms of cross-examination; and assumptions about the 'ideal victim' mean that the voice of the woman is distorted in the current law's focus on whether or not the victim consented. That is hardly respectful of her autonomy.

Second, at the heart of our approach is the message that men must take women's sexual autonomy seriously. Our approach highlights the importance of understanding consent in a rich and nuanced way. It therefore encourages and educates about the importance of autonomy. We reject, therefore, any claim that a paternalistic message is sent. There is, however, another way that our proposed law may be seen as paternalistic and we need to address that next.

Practical Paternalism

Imagine a case where D does not reasonably believe that V is consenting to the sexual encounter, but in fact V is consenting.[1] Under our proposal that would still be rape, because the fact V is consenting is irrelevant to the offence. To some that conclusion is paternalistic. It means that the crime of rape is said to be committed, even though V has agreed to the act. Is this not implying that the law knows better than V whether or not rape has taken place?

We do not agree with that and make several points. First, it is notable that under the current law if D reasonably believes that V is consenting, he will not be guilty of rape. That is true whether or not V consents. So, the current law, in those cases pays no attention to whether or not V consents. Our proposal is no different from the current law than that.

Second, it should be noted that the purpose of the criminal law is to determine the blameworthiness of D for conduct which causes wrongs which deserve a criminal censure. As the case of *R v. Hinks* (2000) demonstrates, this can mean a defendant can be justifiable held to account even where the victim has consented. In that case the defendant's conviction for theft was upheld, even though the victim consented. As was recognised in that case, even where a victim is consenting, they may still be objectified or exploited in a way which justifies the conviction of the defendant (Bogg and Stanton-Ife 2003).

Third, it is well accepted as a matter of English criminal law that a justification can only be relied upon if the defendant acted for that justifying reasons. This is commonly known as the Dadson principle (after the case of *R v. Dadson* 1850), where a defendant (a police officer) had a legal justification for shooting the victim, but was unaware of that, and shot the victim out of malice. This principle means that if D kills V, who unknown to D, is about to attack them, D cannot rely on self-defence. Similarly, if the defendant lacks a reasonable belief that the victim is consenting, then he cannot rely on the defence.

Fourth, in a case where D has no reasonable belief in consent and nevertheless has sex with V, he has used V for his own sexual pleasure. He has used

---

1 Such a scenario may depend on understanding consent as a state of mind (see Chapter 4, Section 'The Concept of Rich Consent').

her body as an object, regardless of consent. This is just as true if it turns out that, unknown to D, V consented. As argued in Chapter 4, Section 'What can Justify the Wrong? Consent or Belief in Consent?', it is objectifying use of a woman, which is at the heart of rape and that is there, whatever V's mind-set, if D lacks a reasonable belief in consent.

Fifth, in a case where D does not reasonably believe that V consents, we think that only in the most bizarre of scenarios would V actually consent. This is because it would be extraordinary for V to consent to have sex with D, if she knew that D thought she did not consent. If V knew the truth about D's state of mind, she would not be consenting. And, even if V did consent, she would not be making a complaint or supporting a prosecution. So the scenario at the heart of the objection will simply not arise.

An Objection to the Subject-Object Presentation

Our proposal describes rape as a sexual penetration without a reasonable belief in consent. That focus on the defendant (his act and his state of mind) may be presented as a male perspective to the sexual act. Sex is something that the man does to the woman, with the woman undertaking a passive role. There is no space in this conception for celebrating sexual interaction as a joint endeavour (Marcus 1992; Gardner 2018).

There is something in this criticism. It certainly seems wrong to regard opposite-sex sexual interaction as something a man does to a woman. However, what this objection misses is that our proposal is about a legal defi-nition of rape, not a definition of good sex. The act of rape is an act done by the defendant to the victim in which she is acted on. She does not participate. Her views of the act are ignored. Rose Owes (2024), drawing on Andrea Dworkin's writing, sees rape as representing violent possession. We do not accept, therefore that our description is a 'sex negative' presentation of sex. Rather it seeks (inevitably inadequately) to describe rape. A description of good sex would look very different.

Exaggerated Benefits

One of the main arguments we have used in favour of our proposal is the practical benefits it offers at trial. In particular, it closes off a whole set of questions which a defendant's barrister may seek to argue to discredit the victim. Above we referred to the reaction of the victim to the rape; messages sent to others before or after the rape; the time it took to report the rape and so forth. All of these will be irrelevant because the consent of the victim is irrelevant.

One objection to our approach is that this claimed benefit is exaggerated. While it is true, our proposal will stop lines of questioning based on information which could not have used to form a reasonable belief in consent, it will not stop other objectionable lines of questioning. If a defendant can still seek to rely on past sexual history of which he was aware; what clothes the victim was wearing, and so forth. This is correct, but we emphasise two points.

First, while it does not stop all such objectionable cross-examination, it does restrict it. The judge would clearly be entitled to stop all cross-examination about information of which D was not aware at the time of the rape. But we accept it will not prevent it all.

Second, we emphasise that our proposal takes a strict approach as to the *mens rea*. The defendant's belief in consent must (a) be objectively reasonable and (b) be a belief about consent, richly understood. We trust that a jury, properly directed, would quickly see that relying on the clothes the victim was wearing, for example, would not constitute a reasonable belief in V's consent. Similarly, if V were intoxicated the jury would not accept the defendant's assumptions that any apparent consent was reasonable, because an intoxicated consent cannot be a rich consent.

Thirdly, and most importantly, our approach makes it clear that the starting point is that the defendant needs to establish that he is justified in committing a prima facie wrong. This makes it very clear that, as argued above, assumptions, generalisations and the like cannot be used to provide such a justification.

We do, however, accept that it would be utterly naïve to think that our proposal would resolve all of the current problems with the law on rape. Rape myths find a way of permeating a trial, whatever the direction used by a judge. Our proposals would need to be joined together with a whole host of other proposals, challenging the 'cultural scaffolding of rape'; (Gavey 2005) the pornification of the media; and wider patriarchal messaging. One reform in particular, we would highlight because it is particularly appropriate in connection with our proposal to have specialist rape courts.

Presumption of Innocence

A foundational principle of the criminal law is the presumption of innocence (Kessler Ferzan 2015). It may be argued by some that requiring the defendant to introduce evidence of a reasonable belief is an unjust interference with this principle. We have addressed these issues in Chapter 4, Section 'Burden of Proof and Belief', but make one further point here.

We reject any suggestion that under our proposal the defendant is being asked here to prove a key element of that offence. That would be true if the view that sexual penetration is a prima facie legal wrong was rejected. However, the objection carries no weight if our starting point is accepted. In other words, this objection is, in effect, no more than a rejection of the view that a sexual penetration is a prima facie wrong. It is no more contrary to the presumption of innocence than the conviction of a defendant who pokes someone in the ear and cannot provide a justification for doing so would be. It is not at all unfair to expect a defendant to carry the evidential burden of introducing evidence that could establish reasonable belief, because, as argued above, he should not be engaging in sex without reasonable grounds for his belief.

Unworkable Definition

Perhaps the strongest argument against our proposal is that it sits uncomfortably with the understanding the person in the street has of rape. As the Thames Valley Police (2024) put it, 'What separates sex or affection from rape or sexual assault? The answer is consent'. There is no doubt that the public sitting in the jury will expect to be told that the key issue in the trial will be whether the victim consented. It might, therefore, be suggested that our proposal will depart too far from the colloquial definition or the definition the law has used for too many years.

While we understand this concern, we note that a recent survey found the public had widespread misconceptions about rape. In a study the CPS (2024), widespread misunderstanding about rape and the law were revealed among a study of 3,000 adults. Thirty per cent did not realise that 'Being in a relationship or marriage does not mean consent to sex can be assumed'. Less than 20 per cent were aware that 'few offenders use physical violence'. The legal system should be challenging any erroneous misconceptions a jury will have. Indeed, that study shows that relying on widespread assumptions about what 'consent' is, or should be, could be very dangerous. This must be all the more so given that we know that the current law is failing women so badly.

Those who are still concerned by this issue, but still being broadly sympathetic to our arguments might agree to a specific new offence in addition to rape to cover cases where there was consent, but the defendant was not aware of the consent. It might be argued that in cases where there is weak consent then this does not amount to the full gravamen of rape. We fear, however, there are grave dangers here. Ranking rapes into more serious or less serious in terms of the label used is dangerous. Consider, for example, the case of *R (Monica) v. DPP* (2018), discussed above, where the defendant had decided the victim into believing they were in a genuine relationship, when in fact he was an undercover police officer using the relationship as part of his cover. In such a case, the depth of betrayal and the length of time of their sexual relationship indicates a very deep wrong, even though it might be classified as a case of weak consent.

Overly Burdensome on Men

Our approach has emphasised the importance of obtaining clear, rich consent. However, not everyone will support that. It has been suggested that 'even those sympathetic to clear modes of sexual communication acknowledge that insisting on a specific word to legitimate sex is artificial and unrealistic, given the heterodoxy of intimate signalling' (Gruber 2009). Various reasons may inhibit a woman making a clear statement of 'yes', even though she expresses consent in other ways. The difficulty being that once we accept that conduct or behaviour outside a clear 'yes' is sufficient for consent, we must acknowledge that ambiguity then enters the picture. The claim, in other words, is that we are caught between two rocks. On the one hand, the strict approach we have advocated requiring clear and rich consent can impede on the rights of women who feel uncomfortable about being explicit in their wishes to engage in sex. On the other, allowing men to rely on silence as consent will diminish the protection for women's sexual autonomy.

A rather different argument is that our approach is too 'perfectionist'; that we should not be using the criminal law to punish all conduct which falls short of the highest ideal of behaviour. Hörnle (2023) has emphasised 'the harsh consequences of criminal accusations and convictions call for a non-perfectionist view'. It might be argued that it can be easy in retrospect to identify behaviour which should have alerted D to ask more questions about consent or to realise the consent was not as rich as we require, but to use the criminal law to sanction such behaviour is wrong. Indeed, she proposes limiting rape to cases where V's opposition was manifest, because only then can we be confident that D was so blameworthy that a criminal sanction can be used.

While we understand that argument, we note that in property dealings we expect people to behave up to the standards of the reasonable honest person. We do uphold moral standards there. Lies and exploitation used to obtain property are clearly fraud or theft. We see no reasons why property criminal law should be an area to uphold such standards, but not sexual criminal law. If lies used to obtain property are clearly fraud, why should not the same lies used to obtain sex be rape. If dishonest exploitation can amount to theft, why can't sexual exploitation amount to rape.

That response also applies to another point that Hörnle (2023) makes, namely that there needs to be a sharing of burdens between parties to a sexual encounter. She writes:

Implementing an 'only yes means yes' model in criminal law means that a person may face criminal conviction and sanctions for omitting to ask for clarification. In comparison, the obligation imposed on the disapproving person with a 'no means no' model is a very small burden; thus, this rule of conduct in criminal law can be viewed as fair.

The argument here is that while we have emphasised in this book the obligation on D to obtain V's rich consent, it is reasonable to expect V to take some steps to express her opposition. If we imagine a case where there is a degree of ambiguity: D has invited V back to his flat 'for coffee' and V has agreed. D and V start to kiss. D starts to initiate sexual intercourse. We might hope D should ask for clear consent, but should not V, who has participated in creating the ambiguous situation, be expected to resolve any ambiguity, by expressing a clear refusal? In other words, it might be said, if D has got the wrong end of the stick in thinking V consents, V bears some responsibility by acting in a way which at least indicates they may be interested in sex.

We firmly reject such reasoning. First, there is evidence of victims of sexual assault 'freezing' in terror (Schiewe 2019). The gender issue is important here. A woman who voices her reluctance is risking a violent reaction. A man who seeks clarification is at worse risking disappointment or embarrassment. The two are not in an equal relationship, at least in terms of a male-female sexual encounter. Given the potential gravity of the harms and the imbalance of power within heterosexual sexual encounters, it is not appropriate to seek a balance between the obligations of the parties (Palmer 2020). Second, if the penetration is a prima facie wrong and receiving a penetration is not, then there is another marked difference between the two parties. D is engaging in an act of penetration which, if he has the consent question wrong, will be a major wrong to V. V by not voicing opposition is not, in any sense, doing anything wrong to D. By 'allowing a penetration', V is not wronging D.

Over-Criminalisation and Anti-Carceral Feminist

Abolition Feminists or anti-carceral feminists are an ever-growing group of feminists who are calling for substantive change to the way we respond to criminal wrongs. With a particular focus on violence against women, anti-carceral feminism is a political movement seeking to abolish traditional justice and replace it with a system without the prison (Brown and Schept 2017, 443). The movement has garnered further support in the United Kingdom largely since the Black Lives Matter protests in 2020. Considering its significance in both society and literature, it is important to consider the likely objections and criticisms abolition feminists might have to our proposals.

We commend abolition feminists' motivations and aims; we completely agree that the criminal justice system as it stands is failing women and girls. Indeed, they too demand a shift away from individual responsibility of women and girls and encourage a move towards a sense of collective accountability for one another. Ultimately, the laudable aim of abolition feminism is 'to reduce harm and increase safety and wellbeing for all' (Abolitionist Futures 2024). They believe justice can be secured through community-based solutions to community-based problems as a form of transformative justice to prevent harms.

Anti-carceral feminists have a 'state sceptical agenda' (Masson 2020). Masson (2020, 70) explains, 'anti-carceral feminists have repeatedly drawn attention to the structural violence explicit within state power – instead imagining a transformed conception of justice outside of the confines of the state'. This is where our positions differ despite similar aims. We do not share the state scepticism of anti-carceral feminists. In fact the opposite, we feel that when issues are 'privatised' to families or individuals, the state is merely failing to act. As Masson (2020, 72) puts it 'anti-carceral feminists, unwittingly, mobilise concepts central to neoliberal rationality, specifically freedom from an oppressive state through privatisation'.

Anti-carceral feminists believe justice is not secured through traditional punitive methods. Yet, what justice means to one may mean something different to another. Indeed, a study conducted by McGlynn & Westmorland (2018) demonstrated just that. Labelled a 'kaleidoscope', alternatives to state punishments include 'rehabilitation, prevention of future harm and a sense of public service and accountability' (McGlynn 2022, 4). As McGlynn (2022, 4) puts it, we must recognise that some survivors' perceptions of justice include criminal justice. Of course, anti-carceral feminists suggest that this may be because this is the only known source of justice. Either way, whatever approach adopted, we think it is fair to include a wide and varied form of justice.

It is likely then, that anti-carceral feminists would categorise us as 'carceral feminists' (Bernstein 2007). This is a term given by abolition feminists to those they perceive as 'pro-criminalisation' who 'actively promote criminalization and imprisonment as responses to gender-based violence' (Loney-Howes et al. 2024, 166). Loney-Howes et al. (2024, 166) explains further 'carceral feminist efforts are entangled in a problematic alliance with the state and are complicit in the use of punitive measures to respond to domestic violence and sexual assault or the extended reach of the state in regulating gender-based violence in ways that cause more harm'. It goes without saying that not only do we reject this labelling, but we also reject the binary that it presupposes, offering just two sides of the debate, leading to the 'erasure of nuance' (Masson 2020). Instead McGlynn (2022, 3) proffers 'continuum thinking' the heart of our proposal for change is a reform to the law, to ensure those who are wronged are properly protected. Ultimately, changing the current legislation, would likely result in more prosecutions and convictions. This however, is not necessarily the aim of our proposal, nor should reform to any laws be motivated by convictions. Instead, we hope that in changing the law we make a change in society. A change to attitudes towards women and girls, attitudes towards agency and autonomy, contributing to the creation of a culture where sex can be a mutually beneficial endeavour when both parties richly consent. Moreover, a change to the law will also help us educate young boys and men about what is right, and how better to navigate intimate relationships. We hope that through widespread systemic change and understanding regarding both the potential harms of penetration but also the potential joy of mutually desired sex, could help reduce the significant number of women and girls who are raped and assaulted every year. The state is always acting; it acts through its inaction and privatisation of issues to individual and families. We are calling for positive action to support individuals. This reflects the approach advocated under the Istanbul Convention (Council of Europe 2012). That Convention invites signatories to use wide range of powers to combat violence against women: from civil law to criminal; from education to the provision of refuges. The obligation on the state is to find the package that protects women from violence. Criminal prosecution can be a part of that package, although it can be by no means the only part.

Abandoning Consent

An alternative to our approach, and one with which we have some sympathy would be to abandon consent altogether in the legal definition and focus instead on the defendant's conduct which when accompanied by sex would amount to rape. The best-known proponent of such an approach is Catherine MacKinnon (2016). She proposes a definition of rape as:

> a physical invasion of a sexual nature under circumstances of threat or use of force, fraud, coercion, abduction, or of the abuse of power, trust, or a position of dependency or vulnerability.

This approach chimes with some of the themes in this book. It avoids the focus being on the victim and, instead, puts the spotlight on the defendant. MacKinnon explains that one if aims is to focus on the concept of 'unequal sex' rather than 'unwanted sex'. While having much sympathy for this approach, we are concerned that inevitably there will be gaps in such a list of behaviours which will indicate consent. A concern may be raised by a case like *R v. Olugboja* (1982), where the defendant approached a victim after a part and asked for sex. She was terrified and allowed the sex to take place. In that case, although it was clear the victim did not consent, the defendant did not threaten the victim or do anything that might constitute an abuse. We are concerned too that cases of coercive control of the kind Zaccour (2023) explores, where the submission of the victim within a controlling relationship will not obviously be captured. A final concern is that the concept of rich consent gives us some criteria in drawing the lines between cases, where referring to simply 'fraud' gives us no marker as to what kind of fraud is likely to lead to a rape charge.

Chapter 7

CONCLUSION

The radical proposal we set out in this book is that rape should be redefined to be a sexual penetration without a reasonable belief in consent, richly understood. Crucially, this means that the consent of the victim is irrelevant to whether or not there is rape. We have argued for the claim that a sexual penetration should be seen as a prima facie legal wrong, which requires a justification. Only a reasonable belief of the defendant that the victim has provided rich consent can provide that justification. In formal legal terms, the *actus reus* of rape would be a sexual penetration and the *mens rea* would be an intention to penetrate. The reasonable belief in consent, richly understood, would be a defence for the defendant to raise, with him carrying an evidential burden of proof. The impact of this would be that in the trial, the spotlight would be on the defendant, and he must explain what justified him to engage in the penetration.

We appreciate this appears to be a shocking proposal, but we hope to have justified it in the previous chapters. For now, we highlight two key advantages. First, it means that at the trial, the focus is on the defendant: what he did, and the justification he had for acting as he did. The victim's state of mind ceases to be relevant. Second, it emphasises the responsibility of the defendant. He needs to justify and explain what he did and how he acted.

At one level, the claim that a sexual penetration is a potentially very harmful act and should only be undertaken with a careful assessment that it will not cause harm seems obvious. But it is very different from how sex is generally seen. Back in 1981, Andrea Dworkin (1981) wrote of the assumptions that underpin society:

(1) Women want to be raped; in fact, women need to be raped;
(2) Women provoke rape;
(3) No women can be sexually forced against her will;
(4) Women love their rapists;
(5) In the act of rape, men affirm their own manhood, and they also *affirm* the identity and function of women – that is, women exist to be fucked

by men and so, in the act of rape, men actually affirm the very woman-hood of the woman.

To many, such claims are ridiculous and they nowadays would not overtly be said. But we can see in the 'rough sex defence' cases (Bows and Herring 2022) how they can still ring true today. The presence of belief in rape myths among the public (CPS 2024), reinforced within our pornographied culture, mean that we need a rethink about our approach to sexual relations. The starting point, we have suggested is that we should see a sexual penetration as a prima facie wrong which the defendant should be prepared to justify, by introducing evidence of a reasonable belief in consent, richly understood. This would challenge the prevalent assumption that sexual penetrations are in their nature good and to be encouraged. Rather they would be recognised as having the potential to do great harm, as well as having the potential to do great good. But the good will only be achieved based on an attitude of respect towards a partner's sexual autonomy.

As we said in Chapter 1, we recognise that changing the substantive law on rape is only one piece of the jigsaw in producing an effective societal response to rape. Clearly, education; combatting pornography; challenging attitudes; changing rules of evidence; finding better support for victim-survivors are all required as well. Adopting our proposed redefinition of rape is an important starting point on that journey. But what we must do, no matter what reforms are made, is shift the spotlight away from the victim onto the defendant.

REFERENCES

Abolitionist Futures. 2024. *Addressing Gender-Based Violence: Carceral Reforms vs Abolitions Strategies*. London: Aoblitionist Futures.

Affirmative Consent. 'Affirmative Consent'. Accessed 6 January 2025. https://cpblondon .com/affirmative-consent-uk/.

Alvarez, Maria. 2017. 'Reasons for Action: Justification, Motivation, Explanation'. In *The Stanford Encyclopedia of Philosophy*, edited by Edward Zalta. Stanford: Standford University.

Alencar, Ticiana. 2021. 'Conditional Consent and Sexual Crime: Time for Reform?' *Journal of Criminal Law* 85: 455–465.

Baron, Marcia. 2017. 'Justification, Excuse, and the Exculpatory Power of Ignorance'. In *Perspectives on Ignorance from Moral and Social Philosophy*, edited by Rik Piles. Abingdon: Routledge.

BBC. 2005. 'Girls Reveal Abuse by Boyfriends'. 21st March 2005 http://news.bbc.co.uk /1/hi/uk/4366167.stm.

BBC. 2012. 'West Mercia Police Apologise Over Rape Campaign Poster'. 2 August 2012. https://www.bbc.com/news/uk-england-hereford-worcester-19091566.

Bernstein, Elizabeth. 2007. 'The Sexual Politics of the "New Abolitionism"'. *Differences* 18(3): 128–151.

Bogg, Alan and Stanton Ife, John. 2003. 'Protecting the Vulnerable: Legality, Harm and Theft'. *Legal Studies* 23(3): 402–422.

Bows, Hanna and Herring, Jonathan. 2022. *Rough Sex and the Criminal Law*. York: Emerald Publishing.

Brown, Michelle and Schept, Judah. 2017. 'New Abolition, Criminology and a Critical Carceral Studies'. *Punishment & Society* 19(4): 440–462.

Brownmiller, Susan. 1975. *Against Our Will: Men, Women and Rape*. London: Fawcett.

Buchanan, James. 1970. 'In Defense of Caveat Emptor'. *University of Chicago Law* 39(1): 64–119.

Christie, Nils. 1986. 'The Ideal Victim'. In *From Crime Policy to Victim Policy*, edited by Ezzat Fattah. London: Palgrave Macmillan.

Clough, Amanda. 2019. 'Finding the Balance: Intoxication and Consent'. *Liverpool Law Review* 40: 49–64.

Collins, Jennifer. 2013. 'The Contours of Vulnerability'. In *Vulnerabilities, Care and Family Law*, edited by Julie Wallbank and Jonathan Herring. Abingdon: Routledge.

Connaghan, Joanne. 2019. 'The Essence of Rape'. *Oxford Journal of Legal Studies* 35: 151–182.

Connaghan, Joanne and Russell, Yvette. 2023. *Sexual History Evidence and the Rape Trial*. Bristol: Bristol University Press.

Council of Europe. 2012. *Convention On Preventing and Combating Violence Against Women and Domestic Violence* (CETS No. 210)). Brussels: Council of Europe.

Craig, Elaine. 2018. *Putting Trials on Trial: Sexual Assault and the Failure of the Legal Profession*. Montreal: McGill- Queens University Press.

Crown Prosecution Service. 2024. *Research into the Public Understanding of Rape and Serious Sexual Offences (RASSO) and Consent*. London: Crown Prosecution Service.

Daly, Ellen. 2022. *Rape, Gender and Class: Intersections in Courtroom Narratives*. Amsterdam: Springer.

Devon and Cornwall Police, Spiking. Accessed 6th January 2025. https://www.devon -cornwall.police.uk/spiking.

Dougherty, Tom. 2021a. 'Deception and Consent'. In *Routledge Handbook of the Ethics of Consent*, edited by in Peter Schaber and Andreas Müller. Abingdon: Routledge.

Dougherty, Tom. 2021b. *The Scope of Consent*. Oxford: Oxford University Press.

Dowds, Elaine. 2020. 'Towards a Contextual Definition of Rape: Consent, Coercion and Constructive Force'. *Modern Law Review* 83: 85.

Duff, Anthony. 2005. 'Strict Liability, Legal Presumptions, and the Presumption of Innocence'. In *Appraising Strict Liability*, edited by Andrew P. Simester. Oxford: Oxford University Press.

Dunn, Jennifer. 2005. '"Victims" and "Survivors": Emerging Vocabularies of Motive for "Battered Women Who Stay"'. *Sociological Inquiry* 75(1): 1–30.

Dworkin, Andrea. 1981. *Pornography: Men Possessing Women*. London: The Women's Press.

Ellison, Louise and Munro, Vanessa. 2009. 'Reacting to Rape: Exploring Mock Jurors' Assessments of Complainant Credibility'. *British Journal of Criminology* 49: 202–234.

Ellison, Louise and Munro, Vanessa. 2010. 'A Stranger in the Bushes, or an Elephant in the Room? Critical Reflections upon Received Rape Myth Wisdom in the Context of a Mock Jury Study'. *New Criminal Law Review* 13(4): 781–801.

Ellison, Louise and Munro, Vanessa 2009. 'Of Normal Sex and Real Rape: Exploring the Use of Socio-Sexual Scripts in (mock) Jury Deliberations'. *Socio & Legal Studies* 18(3): 291–312.

Equality Now. 2017. *The World's Shame – The Global Rape Epidemic: How Laws Around the World are Failing to Protect Women and Girls from Sexual Violence*. London: Equality Now.

Finch, Emily and Munro, Vanessa. 2005. 'Juror Stereotypes and Blame Attribution in Rape Cases Involving Intoxicants: The Findings of a Pilot Study'. *The British Journal of Criminology* 45: 25–38.

Fineman, Martha. 2017. 'Vulnerability and Inevitable Inequality'. *Oslo Law Review* 4: 133–165.

Frey, Ronald and Douglas, Peter. 1992. 'What is it that Makes Men Do the Things they Do Without Consent'. *Confronting Adult Sexual Violence*: 241–251.

Gardner, John. 2009. *Offences and Defences*. Oxford: Oxford University Press.

Gardner, John. 2010. 'Justification under Authority'. *Canadian Journal of Law and Jurisprudence* 23: 71.

Gardner, John. 2018. 'The Opposite of Rape'. *Oxford Journal of Legal Studies* 38: 48–71.

Gardner, Simon. 1991. 'Rape and Inconsiderate Rape'. *Criminal Law Review*, 172–186.

Gathings, Martha and Parrotta, Kylie. 2013. 'The Use of Gendered Narratives in the Courtroom: Constructing an Identity Worthy of Leniency'. *Journal Contemporary Ethnography* 42(4): 668–692.

Gavey, N. 2005. *Just Sex? The Cultural Scaffolding of Rape*. Abingdon: Routledge.

Gilson, Erinn. 2014. *The Ethics of Vulnerability: A Feminist Analysis of Social Life and Practice*. Abingdon: Routledge.

Glidon, Mary. 2024. 'Speech to the House of Commons'. Accessed 6th January 2025. https://hansard.parliament.uk/commons/2024–12-16/debates/B0289156-AB ED-47DF-8AB1-C8BB1CC2D91E/VictimsOfSexualViolenceCourtDelays.

Goodin, Robert. 1985. *Protecting the Vulnerable*. Chicago: Chicago University Press.

Gotell, Lise. 2008. 'Rethinking Affirmative Consent in Canadian Sexual Assault Law: Neoliberal Sexual Subjects and Risky Women'. *Akron Law Review* 41(3): 865–914.

Greasley, Kate. 2021. 'Sex, Reasons, Pro Tanto Wronging, and the Structure of Rape Liability'. *Criminal Law and Philosophy* 15(1): 159–176.

Greenawalt, Kent. 1984. 'The Perplexing Borders of Justification and Excuse'. *Columbia Law Review* 84: 1897–1927.

Gruber, Aya. 2009. 'Rape, Feminism, and the War on Crime'. *Washington Law Review* 84: 581–621.

Gunby, Clare, Carline, Anna, Bellis, Mark, and Beynon, Mark. 2012. 'Gender Differences in Alcohol Related Non-consensual Sex'. *BMC Public Health* 12: 216–219.

Hamer, David. 2007. 'The Presumption of Innocence and Reverse Burdens: A Balancing Act'. *Cambridge Law Journal* 66: 142–173.

Healey, Richard. 2019. 'Consent, Rights, and Reasons for Action'. *Criminal Law and Philosophy* 13: 499–513.

Helm, Rebecca. 2023. 'Constructing Truth in the Jury Box in Serious Sexual Offence Cases'. *Criminal Law Review*: 399–412.

Helm, Toby, 2025. 'Labour Goes Slow on Rape Courts Pledge Amid Fears Over Shortage of Lawyers'. *The Guardian*. 4 January 2025. https://www.theguardian.com /society/2025/jan/04/labour–retreats-on-rape-courts-pledge-amid-fears-over-sho rtage-of-lawyers.

Herring, Jonathan. 2005. 'Mistaken Sex'. *Criminal Law Review*: 511–527.

Herring, Jonathan. 2009. 'Relational Autonomy and Rape'. In *Regulating Rape*, edited by Shelley Day Sclater, Fatemah Ebtehaj, Emily Jackson, and Martin Richards. Oxford: Hart.

Herring, Jonathan. 2016. 'Consent in the Criminal Law: The Importance of Relationality and Responsibility'. In *General Defences in Criminal Law*, edited by Alan Reed and Michael Bohlander. London: Taylor and Francis.

Herring, Jonathan. 2019. *Law and the Relational Self*. Cambridge: Cambridge University Press.

Herring, Jonathan. 2022. 'Coercive Control and Rough Sex'. In *Rough Sex and the Criminal Law: Global Perspectives*, edited by Hannah Bows and Jonathan Herring. York: Emerald Publishing.

Herring, Jonathan. 2023a. 'Consent Mistaken'. In *Reforming the Relationship between Sexual Consent, Deception and Mistake*. Bristol: Criminal Law Reform Now Network.

Herring, Jonathan. 2023b. 'Rethinking Sexual Crimes'. *Anatomia Do Crime* 17: 19–38.

Herring, Jonathan and Madden Dempsey, Michelle. 2010. 'Rethinking the Criminal Law's Response to Sexual Penetration'. In *Rethinking Rape Law: International and Comparative Perspectives*, edited by Claire McGlynn and Vanessa Munro. London: Taylor and Francis.

Herring and McCormack. 2025. 'Reforming Rape: From Consent to Responsibility'. *Gender and Justice*. https://doi.org/10.1332/30333660Y2025D000000010.

Hörnle, Tatjana. 2023. 'The Challenges of Designing Sexual Assault Law'. In *Sexual Assault*, edited by Tatjana Hörnle. Oxford: Oxford University Press.

Humphreys, Terry and Brousseau, Melanie. 2010. 'The Sexual Consent Scale—Revised: Development, Reliability, and Preliminary Validity'. *Journal of Sexual Research* 47: 420–428.

Hymas, Charles. 2024. '14-year-old Girls Report Rape More than Any other Age Group'. *Daily Telegraph.* 20th September 2024. https://www.telegraph.co.uk/news/2024/09/20/14-year-old-girls-most-common-group-report-rape/.

Jagielski, Christina, Hawley, Sarah, Corbin, Kimberly, Weiss, Marisa, and Griggs, Jennifer. 2012. 'A Phoenix Rising: Who Considers Herself a "Survivor" after a Diagnosis of Breast Cancer?' *Journal of Cancer Survivorship* 6(4): 451–457.

Kessler Ferzan, Kimberly. 2015. 'Consent, Culpability, and the Law of Rape'. *Ohio State Journal of Criminal Law* 13(1): 397–445.

Kukla, Rebecca. 2018. 'That's What She Said: The Language of Sexual Negotiation'. *Ethics* 129: 70–92.

Larson, Stephanie. 2018. 'Survivors, Liars, and Unfit Minds: Rhetorical Impossibility and Rape Trauma Disclosure'. *Hypatia* 33: 681–699.

Law Commission. 2023. *Evidence in Sexual Offences Prosecutions. Consultation Paper.* London: Law Commission.

Leahy, Susan. 2014. '"No Means No", but Where's The Force? Addressing the Challenges of Formally Recognising Non-Violent Sexual Coercion as a Serious Criminal Offence'. *Journal of Criminal Law* 78: 309–320.

Lees, Sue. 2002. *Carnal Knowledge: Rape on Trial.* London: The Women's Press.

Loney-Howes, Rachel, Longbottom, Marlene, and Fileborn, Bianca. 2024. 'Gender-Based Violence and Carceral Feminism in Australia: Towards Decarceral Approaches'. *Feminist Legal Studies* 32: 163–185.

MacKinnon, Catherine. 1989. 'Sexuality, Pornography and Method: Pleasure under Patriarchy'. *Ethics* 99(2): 314–346.

Madden Dempsey, Michelle. 2013. 'Victimless Conduct and the Volenti Maxim: How Consent Works'. *Criminal Law & Philosophy* 7: 11–37.

Madden Dempsey, Michelle. 2023. 'The Normative Force of Consent in Moral, Political, and Legal Perspective'. In *Sexual Assault*, edited by Tatjana Hörnle. Oxford: Oxford University Press.

Madden Dempsey, Michelle and Herring, Jonathan. 2007. 'Why Sexual Penetration Requires Justification'. *Oxford Journal of Legal Studies* 27(3): 467–495.

Madhloom, Omar. 2019. 'Deception, Mistake and Non-Disclosure: Challenging the Current Approach to Protecting Sexual Autonomy'. *Northern Ireland Legal Quarterly* 70: 203.

Makenzie, Catorina and Rogers, Wendy. 2013. 'Autonomy, Vulnerability and Capacity: A Philosophical Appraisal of the Mental Capacity Act'. *International Journal of Law in Context* 9(1): 37–67.

Marcus, Sharon. 1992. 'Fighting Bodies, Fighting Words: A Theory and Politics of Rape Prevention'. In *Feminists Theorize the Political*, edited by Judith Butler and Joan Wallace Scott. New York: Routledge.

Mason, Elinor. 2021. Rape, Recklessness, and Sexist Ideology'. In *Agency, Negligence and Responsibility*, edited by George I. Pavlakos and Veronica Rodriguez-Blanco. New York: Cambridge University Press.

Masson, Amy. 2020. 'A Critique of Anti-Carceral Feminism'. *Journal of International Women's Studies* 21(3): 64–76.

Matoesian, Gregory. 1995. *Reproducing Rape: Domination through Talk in the Courtroom*. Cambridge: Polity Press

McConnell, Terrence. 2019. 'When is Consent Required'. *Criminal Law and Philosophy* 13: 283–307

McCormack, Sorcha and Herring, Jonathan. 2024a. 'The Duties of Penetration and the Limits of Consent'. *Criminal Law Review*: 94–103.

McCormack, Sorcha and Herring, Jonathan. 2024b. 'Is Affirmative Consent the Answer? Yes, Sort Of, Maybe'. *Journal of Criminal Law*. https://doi.org/10.1177 /00220183241283212.

McGlynn, Clare. 2018. 'Challenging the Law on Sexual History Evidence: A Response to Dent and Paul'. *Criminal Law Review* 3: 216–228.

McGlynn, Clare. 2022. 'Challenging Anti-carceral Feminism: Criminalisation, Justice and Continuum Thinking'. *Women's Studies International Forum* 93: 1–8.

McGlynn, Clare and Westmarland, Nicole. 2018. 'Kaleidoscopic Justice: Sexual Violence and Victim-Survivors' Perceptions of Justice'. *Social and Legal Studies* 28: 179–201

McKinnon, Catherine. 2016. 'Rape Redefined'. *Harvard Law and Policy Review* 10(1): 431–468.

Molina, Julian and Poppleton, Sarah. 2020. *Rape Survivors and the Criminal Justice System*. London: Victims Commissioner.

Morgan, Robert. 2021. 'What Makes an Attack Sexual?' *Journal of Applied Philosophy* 38(3): 518–534

Morgan, Robin. 1977. *Going Too Far*. New York: Random Books.

Morgan, Mary. 2024. 'Words from an Unideal Victim'. Accessed 6th January 2025. https://shame.bbk.ac.uk/blog/words-from-an-unideal-victim-by-mary-morgan/.

Müller, Andreas. 2018. 'Moral Obligations and Consent'. In *Routledge Handbook of the Ethics of Consent*, edited by in Peter Schaber and Andreas Müller. Abingdon: Routledge.

Munro, Vennessa. 2008. 'Constructing Consent: Legislating Freedom and Legitimating Constraint in the Expression of Sexual Autonomy'. *Akron Law Review* 41(4): 923–987.

Munro, Vanessa. 2017. 'Shifting Sands? Consent, Context and Vulnerability in Contemporary Sexual Offences Policy in England and Wales'. *Social and Legal Studies* 26(4): 417–440.

Naffine, Ngaire. 2020. *Criminal Law and the Man Problem*. Oxford: Oxford University Press.

Nedelskey, Jennifer. 2013. *Law's Relations*. Oxford: Oxford University Press.

Nussbaum, Martha. 2017. 'Accountability in an Era of Celebrity: Sexual Violence, Culture and the Law'. 3 August 2017. https://www.abc.net.au/religion/accountability-in-an -era-of-celebrity-sexual-violence-culture-an/10095542.

NSPCC. 2024. *Child Sexual Abuse*. London: NSPCC.

Owen, Rose. 2024. '"A New Kind of Death": Rape, Sex, and Pornography as Violence in Andrea Dworkin's Thought'. *Political Theory* 52: 1–28.

ONS. 2023. *Sexual Offences in England and Wales Overview: Year ending March 2022*. London: ONS.

Palmer, Tanya. 2020. 'Failing to See the Wood for the Trees: Chronic Sexual Violation and Criminal Law'. *Journal of Criminal Law* 84: 573–589.

Pollard, Paul. 1992. 'Judgments about Victims and Attackers in Depicted Rapes: A Review'. *British Journal of Social Psychology* 31(4): 307–326.

Rape Crisis. 2024a. *Breaking Point*. London: Rape Crisis

Rape Crisis. 2024b. *The Decriminalisation of Rape*. London: Rape Crisis.

Rape Crisis. 2024c. *The 5 Fs: Fight, Flight, Freeze, Flop and Friend*. London: Rape Crisis.

Raz, Jospeh. 1994. *Ethics in the Public Domain*. Oxford: Oxford University Press.

Renzo, Massimo. 2022. 'Defective Normative Powers: The Case of Consent'. *Journal of Practical Ethics* 10(1): 19–31.

Richardson, Deborah and Campbell, Jennifer. 1982. 'Alcohol and Rape: The Effect of Alcohol on Attributions of Blame for Rape'. *Personal & Social Psychology Bulletin* 8(3): 468–476.

Right to Equality. 2024. 'Affirmative Consent'. Accessed 6th January 2025. https://righttoequality.org/campaign/affirmative-consent/.

Savauger, Melissa, Hysock Witham, Dana, and Shinberg, Diane. 2013. 'No Stranger in the Bushes: The Ambiguity Of Consent and Rape In Hook Up Culture'. *Sex Roles* 68: 629–633.

Schiewe, Moriah. 2019. 'Tonic Immobility: The Fear–Freeze Response as a Forgotten Factor in Sexual Assault Laws'. *DePaul Journal of Women Gender and the Law* 8: 1–18.

Schuller, Regina and Stewart, Anne. 2000. 'Police Responses to Sexual Assault Complaints. The Role of Perpetrator/Complainant Intoxication'. *Law and Human Behaviour* 24(5): 535–551.

Scottish Government. 2023. *Victims, Witnesses, and Justice Reform (Scotland) Bill*. Edinburgh: Scottish Government.

Sims, Calvin, Noel, Nora, and Maisto, Stephen. 2007. 'Rape Blame as a Function of Alcohol Presence and Resistance Type'. *Addictive Behaviours* 32: 2766–2775.

Sinclair, Olivia. 2022. 'The Attrition Problem: The Role of Police Officer's Decision Making In Rape Cases'. *Journal of Investigative Psychology and Offender Profiling* 19(3): 135–150.

Smith, Olivia and Skinner, Tina. 2017. 'How Rape Myths are Used and Challenged in Rape and Sexual Assault Trials'. *Social & Legal Studies* 26(4): 411–466.

Stephenson, Laura, Tzani, Calli, Ioannou, Maria, Synnott, John, Williams, Thomas, and Morelli, M.ara. 2023. 'No One Believed Me, and I Have No proof': An Exploration into the Experiences of Spiking Victims'. *Deviant Behavior* 45(5): 642–655.

Stoljar, Natalie. 2017. 'Relational Autonomy and Perfectionism'. *Moral Philosophy and Politics* 4(1): 27–58.

Sweet, Paige. 2019. 'The Sociology of Gaslighting'. *American Sociological Review* 84(5): 851–875.

Temkin, Jennifer. Gray, Jacqueline, and Barrett, Jastine. 2018. 'Different Functions of Rape Myth use in Court: Findings From A Trial Observation Study'. *Feminist Criminology* 13(2): 205–226.

Thames Valley Police, Advice. Accessed 6th January 2025. https://www.thamesvalley.police.uk/ro/report/rsa/alpha-v1/advice/rape-sexual-assault-and-other-sexual-offences/consent/.

Toit, Louise du. 2009. *A Philosophical Engagement with Rape: The Making and Unmaking of the Feminine Self*. Abingdon: Routledge.

United Nations Women. 2024. *Facts and Figures: Ending Violence Against Women*. Geneva: United Nations Women.

Victim Support. 2024. *Suffering for Justice*. London: Victim Support.

Wall, Jesse. 2015. 'Sexual Offences and General Reasons not to have Sex'. *Oxford Journal of Legal Studies* 35(3): 777–804.

Wall, Jesse. 2017. 'Being Yourself: Authentic Decision-Making and Depression'. In *Depression and the Law*, edited by Charles Foster and Jonathan Herring. Oxford: Oxford University Press.

Wall, Jesse. 2019. 'Justifying and Excusing Sex'. *Criminal Law and Philosophy* 13(1): 283–292.

Zaccour, Suzanne. 2023. *But If You Can't Rape Your Wife, Who Can You Rape?' Toward A Course-Of-Conduct Offence Centring Partner Sexual Coercion In Canada*. Oxford: University of Oxford.

CASES

INDEX

www.ingramcontent.com/pod-product-compliance
Lightning Source LLC
Chambersburg PA
CBHW031447280326
41927CB00037B/384